108 Yoga Themes

Transformative Classes, Sequence Ideas,
and Scripts for Teachers & Students

Ava Redfern

contained within this document, including, but not limited to, errors, omissions, or inaccuracies.

Table of Contents

Introduction

Between chaos and calm, there exists a timeless practice that transcends the boundaries of the physical and stretches into the realms of the mind and spirit. Yoga, an ancient art and science, is not merely a series of postures, but a profound journey inward—an exploration of the self, an odyssey towards holistic well-being.

Yoga is the thread that weaves together the physical, mental, and spiritual dimensions of our existence. It is not merely a series of postures to contort the body into, nor is it confined to the four corners of a yoga mat. Rather, yoga is a holistic practice that invites us to step into the fullness of our being, cultivating harmony between the body, mind, and soul.

Imagine yoga as a sacred dance—a symphony of breath, movement, and awareness. It is a practice that transcends the limitations of the physical form, inviting us to explore the subtle realms of consciousness. At its core, yoga is a journey inward, an opportunity to peel away the layers that veil our true nature and connect with the essence of who we are.

For beginners, the practice may initially seem like a series of unfamiliar poses and sequences, but beyond the external postures lies a transformative journey. The magic of yoga lies in its adaptability; it meets you where you are. Whether you are a seasoned practitioner or stepping onto the mat for the first time, yoga offers a sanctuary for self-discovery.

Physical Well-Being

The immediate benefits of a yoga sequence are often felt in the body. As you move through the postures, you engage muscles, enhance flexibility, and improve circulation. The physical postures, or *asanas*, not only build strength and stamina but also release tension stored in the body. This release can bring about an immediate sense of lightness and rejuvenation, leaving you more energized and alive.

Mental Clarity

The rhythm of breath intertwined with movement is the heartbeat of yoga. This synchronicity calms the mind, bringing about a sense of mental clarity. In the midst of life's chaos, the practice becomes a sanctuary where you can cultivate focus, presence, and a deep connection to the present moment. The meditative aspects of yoga guide you into a state of inner stillness, providing a respite from the constant chatter of the mind.

Emotional Equilibrium

Yoga is a journey that extends beyond the mat and into the realm of emotions. As you move through the postures, you may encounter moments of challenge or discomfort. In facing these challenges with breath and awareness, you develop resilience. Over time, the practice becomes a mirror reflecting your emotional landscape, allowing you to navigate it with grace and balance. Yoga becomes a sanctuary for emotional release and healing.

The beauty of yoga lies not only in the immediate sense of well-being that follows a practice, but also in the profound long-term effects that unfold with dedication and consistency.

As you embark on this transformative journey through the pages of this book, remember that the essence of yoga lies not in perfection but in practice. Each breath, each posture, is an opportunity for growth and self-discovery. Through the ebb and flow of the practice, may you find the courage to explore the depths of your being and uncover the boundless potential that resides within. The magic is in the journey, and the journey is yours to embrace.

A well-designed sequence is flexible and adaptable. Understanding the foundation allows you to modify and tailor practices to meet the diverse needs of your students. Whether they seek relaxation, strength, or flexibility, your ability to cater to those needs enhances the overall impact of your teaching.

A yoga class becomes more than just a physical exercise when intentions and foundations are woven into the fabric of the practice. It becomes a sacred space where transformation can occur—a space where students are guided to explore the depths of their being and emerge with a greater sense of purpose and well-being.

Whether as a practitioner or a teacher, consider intentions and foundations as the keys that unlock the full potential of the practice. Embrace the power of purpose, and let the solid foundation be the fertile ground upon which your practice or class blossoms into a sanctuary of self-discovery and transformation. Through intention and foundation, may you cultivate a practice that not only enriches the body but also nourishes the soul.

As I stand at the intersection of over two decades in this industry, my heart resonates with the rhythm of those who have embraced the transformative power of yoga. It's a melody that echoes the harmony of physical vitality, mental clarity, and emotional equilibrium. In the tapestry of my journey as a certified yoga instructor, nutritionist, and naturopath, I have witnessed the astounding potential that lies within each individual to create a life of vibrancy and balance.

This book is not just a manual for teaching yoga; it is a manifesto for cultivating a life steeped in purpose and well-being. It is a call to embrace the essence of yoga beyond the mat, to illuminate the path towards self-discovery and empowerment. It is a testament to the profound impact a mindful and holistic approach can have on our lives, and in turn, the lives of those we have the privilege to guide.

In the words of the great poet Rumi, "The wound is the place where the light enters you." As we embark on this exploration, let us acknowledge that the journey of a yoga teacher is a sacred voyage, a pilgrimage to the depths of one's own being. Setting our intentions and laying a strong foundation are the compass and map that guide us through the intricacies of this inner landscape.

Just as a well-tended garden blossoms with vibrant flowers, so too can our lives flourish when we plant the seeds of intention and cultivate the soil of our minds and bodies. This book is an invitation to dig deep, to unearth the wisdom that resides within, and to water the roots of our existence with the elixir of self-care.

Join me on this expedition into the heart of yoga, where tradition meets modernity, and where the ancient wisdom of the practice intertwines seamlessly with the demands of our contemporary lives. Let us embark on a journey of empowerment, not just as yoga teachers but as individuals dedicated to creating a life that resonates with well-being— a life where the practice of yoga is not just a routine, but a way of being.

Discover the power of self-care, ignite the flame of transformation, and let well-being become the cornerstone of your existence. The odyssey begins within, and *108 Yoga Themes* is your guide to navigating the sacred terrain of your own evolution.

As we delve into the heart of this book, let's start a journey that explores the significance of themes in our practice and teaching. Themes are the guiding stars that illuminate the path of purposeful yoga instruction, offering depth and intention to each class. As we navigate this terrain, remember that themes are not just words; they are the heartbeat of your class—a rhythmic pulse that resonates with the essence of yoga. Join me as we unfold the transformative power of themes and uncover the magic they bring to the practice.

Chapter 1:

What Are Themes and Why Do

They Matter?

In this chapter, we will delve into a fundamental aspect of yoga instruction that has the power to elevate your teaching to new heights—themes. But what exactly is a theme, and why does it matter? In the pages that follow, we will unravel the essence of themes in yoga and explore their significance in fostering a holistic approach to physical, mental, and emotional health. Whether you are a seasoned practitioner or a budding instructor, understanding the art of weaving themes into your teachings can be a game-changer.

What Is a Theme?

A theme serves as the vibrant thread that weaves together the physical, mental, and emotional aspects of the practice. Picture it as the guiding principle that infuses your classes with intention, purpose, and a deeper resonance. But what exactly is a theme in the context of yoga, and why does it play a pivotal role in the journey toward holistic well-being?

At its core, a theme is a unifying concept or idea that forms the essence of a yoga class. It's a dynamic force that transcends the mere sequence of postures, creating a narrative that engages the mind, body, and spirit. Themes can range from profound philosophical concepts to simple, yet powerful, intentions that resonate with the collective energy of the class.

As a certified yoga instructor, I have come to understand that a theme is more than just a philosophical overlay; it is a guiding light that illuminates the path of self-discovery for both the teacher and the student. It is the intentional direction that transforms a series of poses into a meaningful journey—a journey that extends beyond the mat into the fabric of daily life.

Themes can manifest in various forms. They might be inspired by nature, seasons, emotions, or even universal concepts, such as gratitude, compassion, or balance. The beauty lies in their versatility—they provide a canvas for creativity and expression, allowing each class to be a unique exploration.

Themes Can Take on Different Forms

As we delve deeper into the world of themes in yoga, it's crucial to recognize that these guiding principles are as diverse as the individuals who practice them. Themes possess a remarkable ability to take on various forms, adapting to the unique needs, energies, and intentions of each class.

Philosophical Themes

At the heart of yoga lies a profound philosophy that transcends the physical postures. Philosophical themes delve into the timeless wisdom of yogic principles, guiding practitioners to contemplate concepts such as mindfulness, impermanence, and self-realization. These themes offer a transformative journey into the depths of one's consciousness, fostering a connection between the ancient wisdom of yoga and the modern practitioner.

Nature-Inspired Themes

The natural world is a boundless source of inspiration, and nature-inspired themes bring the beauty of the outdoors onto the yoga mat.

Whether it's aligning with the cycles of the seasons, harnessing the energy of the elements, or drawing parallels between natural phenomena and personal growth, these themes invite practitioners to harmonize with the rhythms of the Earth.

Emotional and Energetic Themes

Emotions are an integral part of the human experience, and themes that focus on emotional and energetic aspects can be profoundly transformative. Exploring themes like cultivating gratitude, releasing negativity, or balancing the chakras allows practitioners to navigate the intricate landscape of emotions, fostering emotional intelligence and energetic harmony.

Intention-Based Themes

Sometimes, the simplest intentions hold the most power. Intention-based themes distill the essence of a class into a single, purposeful idea. Whether it's cultivating self-love, finding balance, or embracing the present moment, these themes provide a clear focal point for the practice, guiding practitioners toward a specific state of mind or being.

Storytelling Themes

Narratives have a captivating way of drawing people in, and storytelling themes weave a tale throughout the practice. These themes may involve mythological stories, personal anecdotes, or metaphorical journeys that add a layer of depth and relatability to the class, inspiring both imagination and self-reflection.

Community-Centric Themes

Yoga is not just an individual practice; it is an experience to be lived with a community. Community-centric themes emphasize the power of connection and shared intention. Whether focusing on compassion, unity, or collective growth, these themes create a sense of belonging and encourage practitioners to recognize the interconnectedness of all beings.

Why Does a Theme Matter?

In the world of yoga instruction, themes emerge as not just a creative addition, but as an integral force that breathes life into the practice. Why does a theme matter, and what significance does it hold in the journey toward empowerment and well-being?

Guiding Intention

At its core, a theme provides a guiding intention for the practice. It serves as a compass, directing the energy and focus of the class towards a specific purpose. By establishing a theme, you create a container for the collective intention of the practitioners, fostering a shared experience that transcends the physical postures.

Depth and Meaning

A theme injects depth and meaning into the practice, elevating it beyond a mere physical exercise. It transforms a series of postures into a mindful journey, encouraging practitioners to explore the layers of their being. Themes infuse each movement with purpose, turning the mat into a sacred space for self-discovery and growth.

Connection to Life Off the Mat

The power of a theme extends far beyond the confines of the yoga mat. It bridges the gap between practice and daily life, offering a tangible link to the challenges, joys, and experiences of the real world.

A well-crafted theme becomes a mirror, reflecting insights that practitioners can carry into their everyday existence, fostering a holistic approach to well-being.

Emotional Resonance

Themes tap into the emotional realm, creating resonance that goes beyond the physical. Whether exploring themes of self-love, resilience, or gratitude, practitioners connect with their emotions on a deeper level. This emotional resonance enhances the transformative potential of the practice, facilitating a journey of self-awareness and emotional well-being.

Community Building

Themes foster a sense of community and shared purpose within a class. When practitioners align with a common theme, it creates a supportive environment where individuals feel connected not only to themselves, but also to those sharing the space. This communal aspect enhances the overall experience, promoting a sense of belonging and unity.

Mind-Body Integration

Yoga is a holistic practice that encompasses the mind, body, and spirit. A theme acts as a unifying force, promoting integration and harmony between these elements. By weaving a thematic thread throughout the practice, you guide practitioners toward a more profound understanding of the interconnectedness between their physical, mental, and emotional well-being.

Integrating an Intention

Integrating an intention into your teaching is akin to sowing seeds of purpose that blossom into transformative experiences. As a seasoned wellness practitioner with a dedication to holistic well-being, I understand the profound impact that consciously infusing intention into your classes can have. Let's explore why integrating an intention is a cornerstone in the yoga teacher's toolkit.

Setting the Tone

An intention acts as the tuning fork that sets the tone for the entire class. It is the resonance that echoes through each breath and every pose, creating a cohesive and purposeful flow. By establishing a clear intention, you guide both yourself and your students toward a shared focus, fostering a collective energy that enhances the overall experience.

Mindful Awareness

Integrating an intention encourages mindful awareness throughout the practice. It invites practitioners to bring a heightened consciousness to each movement, creating a bridge between the physical and the mental. As a yoga teacher, you become a guide in this journey of self-awareness, facilitating a space for students to explore the nuances of their thoughts and sensations.

Personal Empowerment

An intention serves as a beacon of empowerment for both the teacher and the students. By consciously choosing an intention, individuals take an active role in shaping their practice. This sense of personal agency extends beyond the mat, empowering practitioners to bring intentionality into their daily lives. As a teacher, you become a catalyst for the transformative potential that lies within each individual.

Aligning With Values

Infusing an intention into your teaching allows you to align your classes with your values and philosophy. Whether it's promoting self-love, cultivating gratitude, or fostering resilience, your chosen intention becomes a reflection of the principles you hold dear. This alignment creates authenticity in your teaching, resonating with students who are drawn to a practice that goes beyond the physical.

Creating a Sacred Space

An intention helps in creating a sacred and mindful space for the practice. It goes beyond the physical postures, turning the mat into a sanctuary where individuals can explore their inner landscapes. This sacred space becomes a container for self-discovery, healing, and personal growth, enriching the overall well-being of your students.

Enhancing Connection

Integrating an intention enhances the connection between the teacher, the students, and the practice itself. It fosters a shared experience, creating a sense of unity and community. As a yoga teacher, you become a facilitator of connection, guiding individuals on a collective journey toward well-being.

Shaping the Sequence

The sequence is the canvas upon which the practitioner paints their yoga experience, and as a certified yoga instructor, you hold the brush that guides this artistic exploration. Let's delve into why shaping the sequence with intention and purpose is a cornerstone in the path toward vibrant health and holistic well-being.

The sequence is not merely a series of physical postures, but a mindful journey guided by intention. By thoughtfully shaping the sequence, you create an immersive experience that invites practitioners to move with awareness and purpose. Each transition becomes an opportunity for self-discovery, turning the practice into a moving meditation.

A well-crafted sequence acts as a visual representation of the chosen theme. It aligns the physical movements with the intended focus, creating a harmonious marriage between the body, mind, and spirit. The sequence becomes a living expression of the theme, allowing practitioners to embody the principles you aim to convey.

The sequence serves as a guide for creating a seamless flow. Smooth transitions between poses and a thoughtful progression of movements contribute to the fluidity of the practice. This flow becomes a dance, allowing practitioners to experience the joy of movement and connection between breath and body.

Shaping the sequence with intention fosters a deepened mind-body connection. The alignment of breath with movement and the purposeful arrangement of postures enhance the somatic experience. Practitioners become attuned to the subtleties of their bodies, nurturing a holistic connection that extends beyond the mat.

A thoughtfully crafted sequence encourages practitioners to explore new possibilities and challenges. By introducing variations and progressions, you create a space for growth and self-discovery. This element of exploration contributes to the transformative potential of the practice, empowering individuals to evolve on their wellness journey.

Remember that each pose, transition, and breath carries the potential to contribute to the holistic well-being of those you guide. Through conscious and purposeful sequence shaping, you become a steward of the transformative power inherent in the practice of yoga.

The Benefits of Theming Your Class

Theming your class emerges as a radiant prism, refracting the transformative power of intention throughout the practice. As a seasoned wellness practitioner, you understand that the benefits of weaving themes into your teachings extend far beyond the mat. Let's explore the multitude of advantages that arise from infusing your classes with purposeful themes.

Enhanced Focus and Mindfulness

Theming your class provides a focal point for both you and your students. It draws attention to a specific concept, intention, or philosophy, fostering a deepened sense of focus and mindfulness. As practitioners align with the theme, each movement becomes a deliberate act, heightening their presence in the moment.

Cultivation of Emotional Intelligence

Themes offer a gateway to emotional exploration and intelligence. By integrating themes that resonate with the human experience—such as gratitude, compassion, or resilience—you create a space for practitioners to connect with their emotions. This cultivation of emotional intelligence contributes to holistic well-being, allowing individuals to navigate their internal landscape with grace.

Connection to a Deeper Purpose

Infusing themes into your classes provides a connection to a deeper purpose. Whether it's exploring philosophical concepts, aligning with nature, or fostering self-love, themes guide practitioners toward a more meaningful engagement with the practice. This connection to purpose becomes a source of inspiration and motivation on and off the mat.

Creating a Unified Experience

Themes act as a thread that weaves through the entire class, creating a unified and cohesive experience. When practitioners collectively engage with a shared theme, it fosters a sense of unity and connection within the class. This shared experience strengthens the sense of community and support.

Encouraging Self-Reflection

Thoughtfully chosen themes invite practitioners to embark on a journey of self-reflection. As they delve into the nuances of the theme, individuals are prompted to explore how it resonates with their personal experiences and challenges. This introspective aspect contributes to self-awareness and personal growth.

Providing Structure and Guidance

Themes offer a structured framework for your class, providing guidance for both you and your students. They act as a roadmap, shaping the sequence, transitions, and overall flow of the practice. This structure adds clarity to the class, enhancing the learning experience for practitioners.

Facilitating Integration of Mind, Body, and Spirit

A well-themed class serves as a conduit for integrating the mind, body, and spirit. Themes go beyond the physical postures, guiding practitioners to explore the holistic nature of their well-being. This integration fosters a harmonious balance that extends into various aspects of life.

Amplifying the Transformative Potential

Ultimately, theming your class amplifies the transformative potential of yoga. It elevates the practice from a series of exercises to a holistic and empowering journey. Themes become a catalyst for personal growth, self-discovery, and the realization of one's fullest potential.

As you continue to explore the art of theming in the pages of this chapter, remember that each theme you choose is a powerful tool for nurturing the well-being of those you guide. Through the intentional weaving of themes, you not only empower your students on their transformative journey but also contribute to the collective radiance of holistic well-being.

As we immerse ourselves in the transformative realm of yoga instruction, we embark on a journey that transcends the physical postures and breathes life into a practice that is both art and science. In this chapter, we explored the essence of themes—those intentional threads that weave a tapestry of meaning, purpose, and connection throughout our classes.

Now, as we turn the page to Chapter 2, we delve into the heart of what it truly means to be a yoga teacher. It's not merely about leading a class; it's about becoming a great yoga teacher—someone who not only imparts knowledge but ignites a spark within each practitioner to illuminate their path toward vibrant health and holistic well-being.

Join me as we navigate the realms of teaching excellence, drawing upon over two decades of experience in the wellness industry. In Chapter 2, we will unravel the qualities and practices that distinguish a yoga teacher. From refining your communication skills to cultivating a nurturing presence, we'll explore the multifaceted aspects that contribute to the art of teaching yoga with impact and authenticity.

So, let's continue this empowering journey, as we transition seamlessly from understanding the significance of themes to embarking on the path of becoming a yoga teacher. It's time to unlock the potential within you and guide others toward the transformative power of yoga with wisdom, compassion, and a genuine commitment to holistic well-being.

Chapter 2:

Becoming a GREAT Yoga Teacher

Yoga is not just a series of postures; it is a holistic approach to life that encompasses the body, mind, and spirit. As an advocate for holistic well-being, I invite you to explore the nuances of being a yoga teacher who goes beyond the conventional, pushing boundaries to create an experience that resonates deeply with each student. This chapter is dedicated to the art of crafting classes that are not just informative but are captivating, transformative, and a journey in themselves.

In the pages that follow, we will delve into the core principles that define a great yoga teacher. It is not just about mastering the *asanas* or memorizing sequences; it is about creating an environment where students feel seen, heard, and inspired to explore the depths of their own potential. We will explore the significance of cultivating a genuine connection with your students, understanding their unique needs, and adapting your teaching style to foster a sense of inclusivity.

A yoga teacher is an artist, harmonizing the elements of tradition and innovation to form a composition that is both classic and modern. We will explore how to infuse creativity into your classes, keeping them fresh, engaging, and attuned to the evolving needs of your students. From incorporating mindful breathing exercises to seamlessly blending different yoga styles, we will unlock the secrets to crafting classes that leave a lasting impact.

Moreover, we will delve into the importance of continuous self-reflection and personal growth as a yoga teacher. The journey to greatness is an ongoing process that requires dedication, openness, and a commitment to evolving alongside your students. By embracing your own vulnerability and authenticity, you empower others to do the same, fostering a community of mutual growth and support.

So, let's embark on this transformative exploration together—a journey that goes beyond the mat and into the hearts and minds of those you guide. Becoming a yoga teacher is not just about teaching yoga; it is about creating an experience that resonates, uplifts, and inspires, leaving an indelible mark on the journey of each student toward holistic well-being.

Curating a New Class Every Time

As we dive into the heart of this chapter, we illuminate the transformative art of curating a new class every time—a practice that not only enhances your teaching but also creates an array of experiences for your students.

Creating a new class with every session is akin to composing a symphony, each posture and transition a note that contributes to the overall harmony. Break free from the shackles of routine, experiment with varied sequences, and let the rhythm of your classes become a dynamic, evolving melody. Infuse the wisdom of tradition with the spontaneity of the present, offering students a chance to explore the uncharted. Just as each student is unique, so should be the experience you craft for them. Delve into the art of tailoring your classes to suit the diverse needs and aspirations of your students. Pay attention to their feedback, be receptive to their energy, and mold your teaching to create an atmosphere where everyone feels seen, supported, and challenged in the best possible way.

While rooted in ancient wisdom, a yoga teacher is also a fearless innovator. Break away from the expected, infuse your classes with elements of surprise, and introduce fresh perspectives that breathe life into tradition. Whether it's incorporating mindfulness techniques, exploring unconventional sequences, or blending different yoga styles, let your creativity be the driving force that keeps your classes vibrant and relevant.

Seamless transitions are the threads that weave a class together into a holistic journey. Cultivate a heightened sense of awareness in guiding your students from one posture to the next. Let the flow of your class mimic the natural rhythms of breath and life, creating an immersive experience where the boundaries between the physical, mental, and emotional dissolve.

Becoming a yoga teacher requires an authentic connection to your own practice. Share your personal insights and experiences, allowing vulnerability to be a guiding light for your students. Authenticity creates resonance, and when your passion for yoga shines through, it becomes infectious, inspiring those around you to explore the depths of their own practice.

Setting an Intention

A yoga teacher understands the profound significance of setting an intention. In this chapter, we delve into the transformative practice of anchoring your teaching in purpose and intentionality, uncovering why this subtle yet powerful act is pivotal on the journey to holistic well-being.

Setting an intention is like finding the heartbeat of your class, grounding your teaching in a meaningful direction. Whether it's cultivating compassion, fostering self-discovery, or promoting mindfulness, the intention becomes the guiding force that infuses every breath, movement, and word with purposeful energy.

An intention acts as a unifying thread, intertwining the diverse elements of a yoga class to create a unified experience. It aligns the physical practice with mental and emotional growth, creating a holistic journey that resonates with your students on multiple levels. This unity fosters a sense of cohesion and connection, transforming the class into a shared exploration of well-being.

In the hustle of everyday life, it's easy to go through the motions without true presence. Setting an intention brings mindful awareness to the forefront, encouraging both teacher and students to be fully present in the moment. This heightened awareness deepens the practice, allowing individuals to connect with their bodies, thoughts, and emotions on a profound level.

Intention acts as a catalyst for personal transformation. As a yoga teacher, your intention becomes a source of inspiration for your students to embark on their own journeys of self-discovery and growth. It empowers them to carry the lessons learned on the mat into their daily lives, fostering a ripple effect of positive change.

An authentic intention reflects your genuine passion and commitment to the well-being of your students. It creates an atmosphere of trust and openness, inviting individuals to engage with the practice authentically. As you share your intention, you invite others to explore the depths of their own aspirations and intentions, fostering a community built on sincerity and mutual support.

Life is a constant ebb and flow of experiences, and a yoga teacher understands the fluid nature of intention. It allows for adaptability, enabling you to respond to the evolving needs of your students and the collective energy of the class. This flexibility ensures that your teaching remains relevant and resonant, meeting individuals where they are on their unique paths.

Setting a Theme

Setting a theme is akin to embarking on a purposeful journey—a thematic compass that guides your class toward a specific destination. This intentional focus infuses your teaching with depth and resonance, providing a cohesive narrative that aligns with the holistic well-being of your students. Each class becomes a chapter in a larger, purposeful story of self-discovery and growth. It unifies diverse elements— postures, breathwork, and meditation—into a cohesive and meaningful experience. This shared focus transforms the yoga studio into a sanctuary where individuals join together in the exploration of a collective theme, fostering a deeper sense of community.

A theme serves as a lens through which your students can mindfully explore various aspects of their practice. It encourages a thoughtful examination of the chosen theme, inviting individuals to connect with its nuances on a physical, mental, and emotional level. This mindful exploration enhances self-awareness, turning each class into an opportunity for personal revelation and growth.

Setting a theme ignites the flame of creativity in your teaching. It encourages you to think beyond the conventional, infusing your classes with fresh perspectives and innovative approaches. Whether the theme revolves around balance, resilience, or gratitude, it invites you to explore creative sequences, incorporate relevant anecdotes, and experiment with diverse teaching methods—all contributing to a dynamic and engaging learning experience.

Themes act as gateways to profound introspection. They invite your students to delve deeper into the layers of their practice and themselves, encouraging a contemplative exploration of the theme's relevance to their lives. This depth cultivates a sense of mindfulness that extends beyond the mat, fostering personal insights and transformative shifts in perspective.

A yoga teacher recognizes the importance of tailoring themes to suit the diverse needs and experiences of their students. Whether teaching a beginner's class or an advanced session, the ability to adapt themes ensures inclusivity, making the practice accessible and relevant to individuals at various stages of their yoga journey.

Picking Something Resonant for Everyone

Setting a theme is a profound act of selecting a resonant note that vibrates through the hearts of each student. The beauty lies in the universality of resonance; a carefully chosen theme transcends individual differences and speaks to the shared humanity that unites us all. It becomes a focal point, a guiding star that aligns diverse experiences into a cohesive journey of exploration and well-being.

A yoga teacher understands the significance of selecting themes that honor the diversity within the class while fostering a sense of unity. Themes can be broad and inclusive, touching on fundamental aspects of the human experience—such as love, gratitude, or self-discovery. This acknowledgment of diversity within unity creates a welcoming space where every student feels seen, valued, and inspired.

Resonance also involves cultural sensitivity and inclusivity. A yoga teacher approaches theme selection with an awareness of the diverse backgrounds and perspectives of their students. Themes can draw inspiration from universal concepts present in various cultures, promoting a sense of unity while respecting the uniqueness of individual experiences.

Themes gain their power when they transcend the mat and become relevant to everyday life. A yoga teacher selects themes that align with the practical challenges and triumphs of their students. Whether addressing stress management, cultivating resilience, or fostering self-compassion, a resonant theme offers tangible tools that extend beyond the studio, enriching the lives of practitioners.

Crafting resonant themes requires an empathetic connection to the experiences and emotions of your students. A yoga teacher listens, observes, and understands the pulse of their class. This empathetic awareness allows you to choose themes that touch upon shared struggles, aspirations, or moments of collective joy, creating a shared narrative that resonates with everyone present.

Language is a powerful tool in setting themes. A yoga teacher employs inclusive language that invites everyone to participate in the theme's exploration. Avoiding exclusivity and embracing words that are universally relatable ensures that every individual, regardless of their background or level of practice, feels invited to engage with the theme.

Talking to Your Students

A great yoga teacher recognizes that language is a potent tool for empowerment. Your words hold the potential to uplift, inspire, and instill confidence. Craft your language with positivity and encouragement, fostering an environment where students feel supported on their unique journeys to physical, mental, and emotional well-being.

The way you speak sets the tone for the entire class. Cultivate a warm and welcoming atmosphere through your words. Use inclusive language that invites everyone to participate, and be mindful of the energy your words convey. A yoga teacher understands that a safe and open environment encourages students to explore their practice with trust and vulnerability.

Mindful communication is about being present with your words. Instruct with clarity, guide with intention, and use language that facilitates a deep connection between the mind and body. Encourage your students to bring awareness to their breath, movements, and sensations, fostering a mindful presence that extends beyond the mat.

Each student brings a unique set of experiences and needs to the mat. A yoga teacher tailors their communication to address this diversity. Be receptive to questions, provide modifications, and offer variations that accommodate different levels of experience and physical abilities. Adapt your language to create an inclusive space where everyone feels seen and supported.

Authenticity is the heartbeat of genuine connection. Share your personal insights, experiences, and challenges with authenticity. Your vulnerability becomes a bridge that connects you with your students, creating a space where real, human connections can flourish. A yoga teacher's authenticity fosters trust and encourages students to embrace their own authentic selves.

The way you speak shapes not only the physical practice but also the emotional and mental aspects of well-being. Foster an environment of self-compassion through your words. Remind your students that yoga is a personal journey, and encourage them to honor their bodies and minds with kindness and patience.

Effective communication is a two-way street. A good yoga teacher listens with presence, offering students the space to share their thoughts, concerns, and experiences. Create an open dialogue that encourages feedback, allowing you to better understand the needs of your students and adapt your teaching accordingly.

Music Selection

Music has the remarkable ability to set the mood and atmosphere of a yoga class. The choice of tempo, melody, and instrumentation can create a sacred space that invites introspection, tranquility, and connection. A great yoga teacher recognizes that music becomes an integral part of the overall experience, influencing the energy and mindset of their students.

The right music can deepen the mind-body connection within the practice. Whether it's the gentle strumming of a guitar during a restorative session or the rhythmic beats of a drum in a more dynamic flow, music becomes a guiding force that aligns breath with movement, fostering a seamless integration of physical and mental elements.

Emotions are woven into the fabric of our experiences, and music has the power to evoke and amplify these emotions. A good yoga teacher understands the emotional resonance of music and selects tracks that resonate with the theme or intention of the class. This creates an emotional landscape that supports self-exploration and the release of tension or stress.

Music can serve as a gentle current that guides the flow of a yoga class. The rhythmic patterns and melodic progression can inspire fluidity in movement, making transitions between poses more seamless. The right musical accompaniment becomes a guiding force, encouraging students to embrace the flow of the practice with grace and ease.

A good yoga teacher curates music that aligns with the journey of the class. Whether guiding students through grounding poses, invigorating sequences, or calming meditation, the music becomes a companion that enhances the narrative of the practice. It creates a cohesive and immersive experience that resonates with the rhythm of the yoga journey.

Music serves as a tool to anchor the mind in the present moment. The carefully chosen soundscape becomes a focal point, supporting mindfulness and focus. A well-prepared yoga teacher uses music as a meditative thread, incorporating it into the essence of the class to inspire students to release distractions and engage wholeheartedly in the practice.

Diversity is celebrated in every yoga class, and the same principle applies to music selection. A yoga teacher considers the diverse tastes and preferences of their students, selecting music that resonates with a broad audience. This inclusivity ensures that the music enhances the experience for everyone, creating a welcoming space for practitioners with varied backgrounds and preferences.

Attention to Detail

Attention to detail is the cornerstone of creating a safe and supportive environment for your students. A good yoga teacher meticulously arranges props, adjusts lighting, and ensures a clean, clutter-free space. These seemingly small details contribute to the overall sense of security, allowing practitioners to fully immerse themselves in the practice without unnecessary distractions or concerns.

Precision in communication is paramount. Verbal cues guide students through the intricacies of each pose, fostering proper alignment and preventing injury. A great yoga teacher hones their ability to articulate instructions with clarity, choosing words that resonate and provide a vivid mental image. Physical adjustments, executed with sensitivity and consent, further refine the nuances of alignment, deepening the practice for each individual.

A yoga teacher is attuned to the diverse skill levels within the class. Attention to detail involves offering modifications for beginners, variations for advanced practitioners, and personalized adjustments for those with unique needs. This adaptability ensures that every student, regardless of experience, feels supported and challenged in their practice.

The sequencing of poses is a meticulous dance, and each transition is a step in a choreographed journey. Attention to detail in sequencing involves considering the logical progression of poses, balancing strength and flexibility, and incorporating intentional breathwork. A yoga teacher crafts sequences with purpose, creating a flow that nurtures the body, mind, and spirit.

Detail-oriented teaching extends beyond the physical postures. A yoga teacher encourages mindful awareness, guiding students to connect with their breath, sensations, and thoughts. By fostering a sense of presence, attention to detail becomes a gateway to the deeper dimensions of the practice—cultivating mindfulness, introspection, and a profound connection to the present moment.

Precision in teaching is an expression of respect for the individual journeys of your students. A great yoga teacher is mindful of personal space, cultural sensitivities, and varying comfort levels. Attention to detail involves creating an atmosphere where everyone feels respected, valued, and encouraged to explore their practice in a way that feels authentic to them.

Attention to detail is a commitment to continuous learning and self-improvement. A good yoga teacher remains open to feedback, seeks opportunities for professional development, and stays informed about advancements in the field. This dedication to refinement ensures that your teaching evolves, staying relevant and inspiring for both you and your students.

Why Being a Great Yoga Teacher Matters

The role of a yoga teacher extends beyond the physical postures and into the realms of inspiration, empowerment, and transformation. Let's explore the profound reasons why aspiring to be a great yoga teacher holds immense significance in the journey toward holistic empowerment.

Guiding the Path to Holistic Wellness

A great yoga teacher is a beacon on the path to holistic wellness. Through the integration of physical, mental, and emotional elements, you guide students toward achieving their best selves. Your teachings become a catalyst for well-being, offering a comprehensive approach that transcends the boundaries of a mere physical practice.

Nurturing Mind-Body Connection

The essence of yoga lies in the connection between mind and body. As a good yoga teacher, your guidance facilitates a profound union between breath, movement, and awareness. This interconnectedness cultivates a heightened sense of mindfulness, leading to a more harmonious and balanced existence for your students.

Empowering Personal Transformation

Yoga is a journey of self-discovery and transformation. Being a good yoga teacher means inspiring and empowering individuals to embark on this personal odyssey. Through your guidance, students navigate the transformative landscapes of their own bodies and minds, unveiling hidden strengths and realizing their full potential.

Fostering a Supportive Community

Beyond the individual journey, a yoga teacher contributes to the creation of a supportive and nurturing community. Your role extends beyond the class, fostering connections among practitioners. Through shared experiences, encouragement, and mutual respect, you become a catalyst for the formation of a community that uplifts and supports each other.

Cultivating a Positive Mindset

The teachings of a yoga teacher extend beyond the mat, influencing the mindset and perspectives of your students. Through intentional language, positive affirmations, and mindful guidance, you contribute to the cultivation of a positive and empowered mindset. This shift in perspective has a ripple effect, influencing every aspect of your students' lives.

Enhancing Emotional Resilience

Life is a journey with its share of challenges and uncertainties. A yoga teacher equips students with tools to navigate these challenges with emotional resilience. Through breathwork, meditation, and mindfulness practices, you empower individuals to face adversity with strength, grace, and a grounded sense of self.

Inspiring a Lifelong Journey of Learning

The journey of a great yoga teacher is a continuous quest for knowledge and self-improvement. By embodying a commitment to lifelong learning, you inspire your students to adopt a similar mindset. This shared dedication to growth creates a dynamic and evolving community that thrives on the pursuit of knowledge and self-discovery.

Leaving a Lasting Legacy

Being a great yoga teacher allows you to leave a lasting legacy in the lives of your students. Your teachings become imprints on their personal journeys, influencing the way they approach challenges, embrace well-being, and cultivate a sense of empowerment. The impact of a yoga teacher extends far beyond the confines of a single class, resonating in the lives of those you touch.

As we navigate the path to becoming a well-prepared yoga teacher, we recognize that the breath is not just the rhythm of life, but a guiding force in the transformative journey we are about to undertake. In the sacred space of a yoga class, the breath becomes the silent orchestrator, weaving together the threads of movement, mindfulness, and empowerment.

Now, as we move to the next chapter, let's explore the profound significance of breathwork—a practice that transcends the boundaries of physical postures. Inhale deeply, exhale fully, and let us delve into the essence of The Importance of Breathwork, a chapter that unveils the transformative power of conscious breathing in the realm of holistic well-being and yoga empowerment.

Chapter 3:

The Importance of Breathwork

Why does the breath hold such significance in the world of yoga? Beyond the mechanics of respiration lies a treasure trove of benefits waiting to be unlocked. Proper breathing not only fuels the body with oxygen but also acts as a bridge between the conscious and unconscious aspects of our being. As we delve into the wisdom of ancient yogic practices, you'll understand how breathwork becomes a potent tool for self-regulation, stress reduction, and cultivating a profound sense of inner peace.

What Is Breathwork?

The term "breathwork" transcends the simple act of inhaling and exhaling. It is a deliberate and conscious exploration of the breath's transformative power—a journey that extends beyond the physical, reaching into the realms of mental clarity, emotional balance, and spiritual connection.

At its core, breathwork encompasses a variety of intentional breathing techniques, collectively known as *pranayama*. Derived from the Sanskrit words "prana" (life force) and "ayama" (extension or control), *pranayama* involves the regulation and expansion of the life force energy through breath. This ancient practice recognizes the breath as a bridge between the body and the mind, offering a pathway to elevate one's consciousness and vitality.

The Three Pillars of Breathwork

Conscious Awareness

At the heart of breathwork lies the simple yet profound act of being fully present with each breath. Conscious awareness involves tuning into the rhythm of your breath, observing its nuances, and cultivating a mindful connection to the present moment. By bringing attention to the breath, practitioners unlock a gateway to heightened self-awareness and a deeper understanding of their inner landscape.

Intentional Regulation

Breathwork is not just about the breath itself, but also about how we modulate it. Through intentional regulation, individuals can influence their physiological and psychological states. Techniques, such as deep belly breathing, alternate nostril breathing (Nadi Shodhana), and the victorious breath (*Ujjayi*) are employed to balance the nervous system, reduce stress, and promote a sense of calm and focus.

Energetic Flow

In the yogic philosophy, the breath is considered the carrier of prana, the vital life force that animates all living things. Breathwork facilitates the smooth flow of this energy throughout the body, removing blockages and promoting vitality. By consciously directing and enhancing the energetic flow, practitioners not only rejuvenate their physical bodies, but also nourish the subtle energy centers known as chakras.

Embarking on the path of breathwork is a transformative odyssey, offering a holistic approach to well-being that extends far beyond the yoga mat. As we delve into the practical aspects of breathwork in the following sections, you'll discover the power that resides in your breath—the key to unlocking a reservoir of untapped potential and cultivating a radiant and empowered self.

Proper Breathwork: Navigating the Rhythms of Vitality

Proper breathwork, or *pranayama*, emerges as a key element in the repertoire of a yoga teacher, offering a gateway to profound physical, mental, and emotional well-being.

The Foundations of Proper Breathwork

Conscious Awareness

The journey of proper breathwork begins with conscious awareness. Before delving into specific techniques, it is crucial to cultivate a mindful connection to the breath. Encourage your students to observe the natural rhythm of their breathing without judgment or alteration. Through this awareness, individuals lay the foundation for intentional breath regulation.

Diaphragmatic Breathing

At the core of proper breathwork lies the practice of diaphragmatic breathing. This technique involves engaging the diaphragm, the primary muscle of respiration, to facilitate deep and expansive breaths. As individuals learn to breathe into their diaphragm, they enhance oxygen exchange, promoting a sense of calm and vitality.

Intentional Regulation

Pranayama is the intentional regulation of the breath for specific outcomes. As a yoga teacher, guide your students in exploring various techniques that suit their needs. Whether it's the calming effects of n*adi shodhana* (alternate nostril breathing) or the energizing quality of k*apalabhati* (skull-shining breath), intentional breath regulation becomes a tool for self-mastery.

The Importance of Proper Breathwork

Stress Reduction and Relaxation

Proper breathwork engages the parasympathetic nervous system, triggering the relaxation response. Encouraging slow, deep breaths soothes the nervous system, reducing stress and promoting a state of relaxation. As a yoga teacher, impart the skill of using the breath as a reliable anchor during moments of tension and uncertainty.

Enhanced Focus and Mental Clarity

The link between breath and mind is profound. By guiding students in proper breathwork, you empower them to enhance focus and mental clarity. Oxygenating the brain through intentional breathing fosters cognitive function, enabling individuals to approach challenges with a calm and centered mind.

Balancing Energy Flow

The breath serves as the carrier of prana, the vital life force. Proper breathwork facilitates the balanced flow of this energy throughout the body. Through techniques such as *Ujjayi* (victorious breath) or *Dirga* (three-part breath), individuals can cleanse energetic pathways, promoting vitality and holistic well-being.

Mind-Body Connection

As a yoga teacher, emphasize the integration of breath with movement. In yoga asana practice, synchronize breath and posture to deepen the mind-body connection. Through this integration, students cultivate a heightened awareness of their bodies and an appreciation for the transformative power of the breath.

Teaching Tips for Proper Breathwork

Begin with Foundational Awareness

Initiate your students into proper breathwork by fostering awareness. Encourage them to observe their natural breath without alteration, creating a foundation for conscious breathing.

Progressive Introduction of Techniques

Introduce *pranayama* techniques gradually, considering the experience and comfort levels of your students. Begin with foundational practices like diaphragmatic breathing before progressing to more advanced techniques.

Emphasize Consistency

Consistency is key to reaping the benefits of proper breathwork. Encourage your students to incorporate conscious breathing into their daily lives, fostering a habit that extends beyond the yoga studio.

Individualized Approach

Recognize the uniqueness of each student and their specific needs. Offer modifications and variations to accommodate different levels of experience and physical conditions.

How to Properly Belly Breathe

Step 1: Find a comfortable posture

Begin by guiding your students to find a comfortable seated or lying posture. Encourage a straight spine and relaxed shoulders. If seated, ensure that their feet are flat on the ground, and if lying down, their knees can be bent or straight, based on comfort.

Step 2: Place one hand on the chest, the other on the abdomen

Instruct your students to place one hand on their chest and the other on their abdomen. This tactile connection provides immediate feedback and helps cultivate awareness of the breath's movement.

Step 3: Inhale slowly and deeply through the nose

Encourage your students to inhale slowly and deeply through their nose. Emphasize the importance of a smooth and controlled inhalation, allowing the breath to fill the lungs.

Step 4: Feel the abdomen expand

As the breath flows in, guide your students to focus on the hand resting on their abdomen. Instruct them to allow the breath to expand the diaphragm and belly outward. The chest should remain relatively still during this phase.

Step 5: Exhale gradually through the mouth

Next, guide your students to exhale slowly and gradually through their mouth. Encourage a gentle contraction of the abdominal muscles as they release the breath. The hand on the abdomen will move inward as the breath is expelled.

Step 6: Repeat the process mindfully

Encourage a rhythmic and mindful repetition of the belly breathing cycle. Inhale deeply, feel the abdomen expand, exhale slowly, and observe the gentle contraction. Emphasize the importance of maintaining a calm and steady pace, fostering a sense of relaxation.

Step 7: Release tension and surrender

As your students continue the practice, invite them to release any tension held in their shoulders, neck, or face. Emphasize the surrendering nature of the exhalation, allowing stress and tension to melt away with each breath.

Step 8: Integrate belly breathing into asana practice

Once your students are comfortable with the basic technique, encourage them to integrate belly breathing into their yoga asana practice. Emphasize the synchronization of breath and movement, creating a seamless flow that enhances the mind-body connection.

Breathing With Poses

As a yoga teacher, guiding students to synchronize their breath with poses is a potent way to deepen their practice and unlock the full potential of yoga. Let's delve into the art of breathing with poses:

Cultivate Breath Awareness

Begin by inviting your students to cultivate awareness of their breath. Encourage them to observe the natural rhythm of their inhalations and exhalations before initiating any movement. This foundational awareness sets the stage for a harmonious union of breath and pose.

Inhale to Expand and Elevate

As your students prepare to move into a pose, guide them to initiate the movement with a slow and deliberate inhalation. The inhale serves as the expansive force, lifting and energizing the body. For example, during a Sun Salutation, encourage an inhale as they reach their arms overhead in a Mountain Pose.

Exhale to Ground and Deepen

The exhale becomes the grounding force that deepens the pose. As your students transition into the posture, prompt them to exhale slowly and with control. This intentional exhalation allows for a sense of surrender, stability, and a deeper connection to the present moment. In a Forward Fold, for instance, the exhale guides the body to fold forward with grace and mindfulness.

Maintain a Rhythmic Flow

Emphasize the importance of maintaining a rhythmic flow between breath and movement. The breath should seamlessly guide the transitions between poses, creating a continuous and fluid sequence. Encourage your students to avoid holding their breath and to instead let the breath be the conductor orchestrating the symphony of their practice.

Link Breath and Alignment

Instruct your students to use the breath as a guide for proper alignment within each pose. As they inhale, encourage a lengthening and opening of the body; as they exhale, suggest a gentle engagement of core muscles and a softening into the pose. This mindful alignment ensures that each breath contributes to the holistic well-being of the practitioner.

Explore Breath Retention

Introduce the concept of breath retention during static poses. In certain asanas, guide your students to hold the breath for a brief moment at the top of the inhalation or bottom of the exhalation. This practice deepens their connection to stillness and cultivates a profound awareness of the present.

Tailor Breath to Intensity

As the intensity of poses varies, encourage your students to adapt their breath accordingly. During more challenging poses, such as a Warrior sequence, remind them to maintain a steady and controlled breath, preventing unnecessary tension or strain.

Incorporate Pranayama Techniques

Integrate *pranayama* techniques into asana practice to enhance the breathwork experience. Techniques like *Ujjayi* breath, *Kapalabhati*, or *Dirga Pranayama* can elevate the energetic and transformative aspects of the practice.

Why It Matters to a Sequence

Breathing with poses anchors your students in the present moment. As they synchronize breath with movement, the mind becomes attuned to the subtle shifts within the body. This mindful presence creates a sanctuary where practitioners can escape the chatter of the mind and immerse themselves fully in the experience of each pose.

The breath is the carrier of prana, the life force energy. When harmonized with poses, the breath becomes a conduit for the flow of this vital energy throughout the body. This energetic flow revitalizes cells, nourishes organs, and ignites a transformative journey within. Each inhale infuses life into the pose, and each exhale releases stagnant energy, creating a dynamic and balanced sequence.

Breathwork with poses enhances body awareness. The breath becomes a guide, signaling the body to expand, contract, and align. This heightened awareness fosters a deep connection between breath and movement, allowing practitioners to explore the edges of their physicality with intention, intelligence, and safety.

The breath serves as a natural guide for alignment within each pose. Inhalations can encourage lengthening and expansion, while exhalations invite a gentle engagement and grounding. This union of breath and alignment not only prevents strain but also promotes a sense of stability and balance, creating a foundation for a safe and sustainable practice.

Breathing with poses strengthens the mind-body connection. As the breath becomes the bridge between thought and action, students cultivate a profound understanding of how their mental and emotional states influence their physical practice. This integrated awareness empowers practitioners to navigate challenges with resilience, grace, and self-compassion.

The breath is intimately tied to emotions. Breathing with poses provides a conduit for emotional release. Encourage your students to use the breath to soften into challenging poses, allowing emotional tension to dissipate with each exhale. This gentle release fosters a sense of emotional well-being and balance.

The rhythm of breath with poses transforms the practice into a moving meditation. As students flow seamlessly between postures, the breath becomes the focal point, guiding them into a meditative state. This meditative flow transcends the physical, offering a profound journey into the meditative aspects of yoga.

Breathing with poses instills resilience. The breath becomes a steady companion during challenging sequences, encouraging practitioners to meet discomfort with a calm and focused mind. In transitions between poses, the breath acts as a thread, weaving coherence and grace into the practice.

Transitions

Transitions offer a unique opportunity to deepen mindful presence. By breathing consciously through the spaces between poses, students anchor themselves in the present moment. The breath becomes a gentle reminder to let go of the past posture and to approach the upcoming one with a fresh, open awareness.

Encourage your students to view transitions as a continuation of the breath and movement symphony. The inhales initiate expansion and preparation for the next pose, while the exhales guide a smooth and controlled descent or ascent. This harmonization enhances the mind-body connection and creates a seamless flow.

Proper breathwork during transitions promotes stability and alignment. As students move between poses, the breath guides them to maintain a strong, centered core. The breath becomes a stabilizing force, preventing unnecessary strain and fostering alignment that supports the body's natural architecture.

Transitions are a gateway to a meditative flow. By breathing consciously, students transcend the physical aspects of the practice, entering a state of moving meditation. The breath becomes a rhythmic mantra, guiding them through the ebb and flow of the sequence with a tranquil mind.

Breathing intentionally through transitions builds resilience and focus. As students encounter moments of challenge or complexity, the breath becomes a source of inner strength. Encourage them to breathe with purpose, meeting transitions with a calm and focused mind, fostering resilience and concentration.

The breath can transform transitions into mindful pauses. As students move through these spaces, the breath becomes a conscious interlude—a brief pause to acknowledge the journey traveled and prepare for the path ahead. This intentional pause allows for reflection and appreciation of the practice's unfolding narrative.

Influence by Different Themes

Each theme introduces a unique lens through which practitioners can explore their breath, bringing intention, emotion, and purpose into their practice. As a yoga teacher, weaving different themes into breathwork elevates the practice beyond the physical, fostering a holistic and transformative journey. Let's explore the influence of various themes on breathwork, paired with corresponding asanas that resonate with each theme.

Grounding and Stability

Theme: connecting to earthly roots.

Breathwork emphasis: Deep, steady breaths to anchor and ground.

Asanas

- Mountain Pose (*Tadasana*)

- Tree Pose (*Vrksasana*)

- Warrior Poses (*Virabhadrasana* series)

Inner Strength and Empowerment

Theme: cultivating personal power.

Breathwork emphasis: Ujjayi breath for inner strength and empowerment.

Asanas

- Warrior Poses (*Virabhadrasana* series)

- Chair Pose (*Utkatasana*)

- Boat Pose (*Navasana*)

Opening the Heart

Theme: embracing love and compassion.

Breathwork emphasis: Heart-opening breaths for love and compassion.

Asanas

- Camel Pose (*Ustrasana*)

- Bridge Pose (*Setu Bandhasana*)

- Upward-Facing Dog (*Urdhva Mukha Svanasana*)

Mindfulness and Presence

Theme: cultivating present-moment awareness.

Breathwork emphasis: Mindful, diaphragmatic breathing.

Asanas

- Seated Meditation (*Sukhasana*)

- Corpse Pose (*Savasana*)

- Mindful Movement in Sun Salutations

Balancing Energies

Theme: finding equilibrium.

Breathwork emphasis: Alternate nostril breathing (*Nadi Shodhana*) for balance.

Asanas

- Tree Pose (*Vrksasana*)

- Eagle Pose (*Garudasana*)

- Dancer Pose (*Natarajasana*)

Breathwork, when intertwined with diverse themes, transforms yoga practice into a dynamic and multifaceted journey. As a yoga teacher, embracing these thematic elements elevates your guidance, offering students a rich and transformative exploration of breath and self-discovery. The marriage of breathwork and themes becomes a powerful vehicle for holistic well-being, empowering individuals to transcend the physical and embark on a profound inward journey.

The rhythmic dance of breath within each pose, transition, and meditative pause is the heartbeat of an empowered practice. It fosters a connection between the physical body and the subtle realms of energy, emotion, and consciousness. But the journey doesn't end here; it evolves into the art of designing and thematic crafting, where the yoga teacher takes on the role of a guide, blending breath, movement, and intention into a harmonious composition.

As we transition to the next phase, we embark on a journey through themes created for each season. Here, we discover the intricacies of creating an immersive yoga experience. Much like a skilled composer arranges musical notes to evoke emotions, a yoga teacher shapes a class that resonates with the essence of breath, guiding practitioners towards physical vitality, mental clarity, and emotional balance.

Chapter 4:

Winter

Winter is not merely a season of frosty landscapes and shorter days; it is a time to turn inward, reconnect with ourselves, and embrace the serenity that lies within.

Within these pages, you will discover 27 carefully curated themes designed to align your yoga practice with the unique energies of winter. Each theme unfolds like a snowflake, offering a delicate and intricate pattern to explore on the mat. We believe that yoga extends beyond the physical postures, breathing exercises, and meditation—it is a harmonious blend of mind, body, and spirit.

Slowing Down: Tuning Into Tranquility

Music: Solfeggio frequencies or meditation music.

Opening script: "In the stillness of winter, we surrender to the gentle cadence of our breath. Let us tune into the wisdom of our bodies and calm the nervous system, inviting serenity to flow through every pose."

Poses to consider:

- Child's

- Happy Baby

- Reclined Swan

- Waterfall

- Corpse

- Sun Salutation

Transitions: Guide practitioners with slow, intentional movements, emphasizing the seamless flow between each pose.

Breathwork coaching: Encourage deep, mindful breaths, syncing inhalations and exhalations with the rhythm of the chosen music.

Closing script: "As we conclude, carry this tranquility within you. May your journey through winter be a dance of peace and self-discovery."

Self-Care: Nourishing From Within

Music: heart-centered frequencies or slow jazz.

Opening script: "In the sanctuary of self-care, we honor the temple that is our body. Let the heart-centered frequencies guide us as we embark on a journey of rejuvenation and self-love."

Poses to consider:

- Falling Star

- Downward Facing Dog

- Camel

- Bow

- Jack in the Box

- Legs Up the Wall

Transitions: Encourage a seamless flow, emphasizing the nurturing quality of each movement.

Breathwork coaching: Guide practitioners to breathe deeply, drawing attention to the expansion of the heart with each breath.

Closing script: "As you conclude this practice, carry the warmth of self-care with you. May you shine from the inside out, a beacon of love and well-being."

Gratitude: Embracing Life's Blessings

Music: uplifting and grateful tunes.

Opening script: "In the spirit of gratitude, we open our hearts to the abundance of life. Even in the winter chill, we find warmth in the little things. Let the music of gratitude guide us."

Poses to consider:

- Tiger

- Chair

- Warrior 1

- Warrior 2

- Warrior 3

- Tree

Transitions: Encourage graceful transitions, symbolizing the interconnectedness of all things.

Breathwork coaching: Guide practitioners to breathe deeply, expressing gratitude with each inhale and releasing any tension with each exhale.

Closing script: "As you bow in gratitude, carry this sense of thankfulness with you. May your winter days be filled with appreciation and joy."

Celebrate the Winter Solstice: Reflecting in Rhythmic Stillness

Music: slow and rhythmic tunes.

Opening script: "As winter's embrace deepens, let us celebrate the stillness of the Winter Solstice. In the quiet rhythm of this season, we find joy and reflection."

Poses to consider:

- Fish

- Bow

- Shoulder

- Locust

- Chair

- Warrior 2

Transitions: Encourage intentional transitions, mirroring the contemplative nature of the winter solstice.

Breathwork coaching: Guide practitioners to breathe rhythmically, syncing breath with the slow beat of the chosen music.

Closing script: "As you conclude this celebration of stillness, carry the peace of the Winter Solstice within you. May your reflections be a source of light in the winter darkness."

Inner Child Happiness: Rediscovering Joy

Music: joyful and nostalgic melodies.

Opening script: "In the playground of our inner selves, let us connect with the child within. May the music of joy and nostalgia guide us in making our inner child feel happy and safe."

Poses to consider:
- Happy Baby

- Downward Facing Dog

- Balancing Butterfly

- Lion's Breath

- Supine Twist

- Twisted Lizard

Transitions: Encourage playful transitions, embracing the spirit of joy and lightness.

Breathwork coaching: Guide practitioners to breathe deeply, inviting a sense of playfulness and freedom into each breath.

Closing script: "As you conclude this journey to happiness, carry the laughter of your inner child with you. May your days be filled with light and joy."

Find Your Inner Light: Illuminating From Within

Music: uplifting and inspirational compositions.

Opening script: "In the depths of winter, we look within to recognize our inner power. Let the music of upliftment guide us as we discover the radiant light that resides within."

Poses to consider:
- Butterfly

- Half Lotus Seated Twist

- Cat/Cow

- Low Lunge

- Downward Facing Dog

- Triangle

Transitions: Encourage fluid transitions, symbolizing the continuous journey of self-discovery.

Breathwork coaching: Guide practitioners to breathe with purpose, allowing the breath to carry the illumination of inner light throughout the body.

Closing script: "As you conclude this exploration, carry the brilliance of your inner light with you. May your path be guided by the radiance of your true self."

Forgiveness: Opening the Heart's Sanctuary

Music: heart-centered frequencies.

Opening script: "In the sanctuary of forgiveness, we open our hearts to the healing frequencies within. Let the music guide us in forgiving ourselves and others, releasing the weight that no longer serves."

Poses to consider:

- Mountain

- Sun Salutation

- Chair

- Warrior 2

- Triangle

- Extended Side Angle

Transitions: Encourage graceful transitions, reflecting the gentle unfolding of forgiveness.

Breathwork coaching: Guide practitioners to breathe deeply, inviting the healing frequencies to wash away any lingering tension.

Closing script: "As you conclude this journey of forgiveness, carry the lightness of an open heart with you. May compassion be your guide in the winter stillness."

At Peace With Yourself: Embracing Acceptance

Music: 528Hz frequencies to stimulate the solar plexus.

Opening script: "In the frequencies of acceptance, we find peace. Let the music guide us as we embrace ourselves, acknowledging what we can't control and loving ourselves regardless."

Poses to consider:

- Easy Pose moving into Forward Bend

- Standing Forward Bend with Shoulder Opener

- Wide-Legged Standing Forward Bend

- Rabbit

- Thunderbolt Pose with Eagle Arms

- Side Stretch

Transitions: Encourage gentle transitions, embodying the fluidity of self-acceptance.

Breathwork coaching: Guide practitioners to breathe with a sense of surrender, allowing the breath to carry acceptance throughout the body.

Closing script: "As you conclude this practice of self-love, carry the peace of acceptance with you. May you find solace in the winter quietude."

Practice Compassion: Radiate the Warmth Within

Music: 639Hz frequencies for the heart, or anything about opening up to love and loving others.

Opening script: "In the frequencies of compassion, we open our hearts to love and warmth. Let the music guide us in sharing compassion with ourselves and others."

Poses to consider:

- Child

- Mountain

- Camel

- Eagle

- Triangle

- Upward Facing Dog

Transitions: Encourage open-hearted transitions, symbolizing the expansive nature of compassion.

Breathwork coaching: Guide practitioners to breathe deeply, allowing the breath to be a conduit for the flow of compassion.

Closing script: "As you conclude this journey of compassion, carry the warmth of love with you. May your winter days be filled with connection and kindness."

Harmony: Balancing the Essence Within

Music: chakra-balancing melodies.

Opening script: "In the harmonies of balance, we seek equilibrium within ourselves. Let the music guide us in finding the symphony that resonates through our lives."

Poses to consider:

- Cat-Cow

- Child's

- Bridge

- Tree

- Warrior 2

- Warrior 3

Transitions: Encourage transitions that symbolize the dance of balance in mind, body, and spirit.

Breathwork coaching: Guide practitioners to breathe with awareness, harmonizing breath with the rhythm of the chosen music.

Closing script: "As you conclude this practice of harmony, carry the balance within you. May your winter be a dance of equilibrium and serenity."

Reflection: Nurturing the Inner Mind

Music: resonating with 963Hz, 852Hz, and 639Hz for the crown and solar plexus chakras.

Opening script: "In the tapestry of winter, let us slow down, embracing the gift of introspection. As we flow through these poses, may our minds become mirrors, reflecting the wisdom within."

Poses to consider:

- Warrior 1

- Mountain

- Cat-Cow

- All Fours with a Twist

- Gate

- Crescent

Transitions: Encourage deliberate transitions, symbolizing the contemplative nature of reflection.

Breathwork coaching: Guide practitioners to breathe deeply, inviting mindfulness into each breath.

Closing script: "As you conclude this reflection, may the insights gained be seeds for personal growth. Winter's quietude is an invitation to listen, understand, and nurture your inner wisdom."

Being Present: Rooted in the Now

Music: resonating with the root chakra at 396Hz.

Opening script: "In the essence of now, let us ground ourselves. As we move through these poses, may our awareness deepen, rooting us firmly in the present moment."

Poses to consider:
- Child

- Standing Forward Bend

- Mountain

- Eagle

- High Lunge

- Upward Plank

Transitions: Encourage mindful transitions, emphasizing the connection between breath and movement.

Breathwork coaching: Guide practitioners to breathe with awareness, grounding each breath into the present moment.

Closing script: "As you conclude this journey into presence, may the roots you've planted anchor you in the richness of each passing moment. Winter's beauty is found in the now."

Creating Warmth: Igniting the Inner Fire

Music: cozy and festive tunes.

Opening script: "Amidst winter's chill, let us find warmth within. Through these poses, may the life force energy in your body kindle a fire, guiding you through the cold months."

Poses to consider:
- Chair

- Boat

- Side Angle

- Plank

- Bridge

- Goddess

Transitions: Encourage fluid transitions, embodying the warmth and vitality of the inner fire.

Breathwork coaching: Guide practitioners to breathe with intention, stoking the inner fire with each breath.

Closing script: "As you conclude this practice of warmth, may the fire within you burn bright, providing sustenance and energy throughout the winter's embrace."

Embrace Stillness: A Dance of Quietude

Music: slow and calm, resonating with 396Hz, 852Hz, and 963Hz.

Opening script: "In the gentle embrace of stillness, let us appreciate the present moment. As we gracefully flow through these poses, may the calm of winter envelop our beings."

Poses to consider:

- Forward Bend and Standing Forward Bend

- Low Lunge

- High Lunge

- Downward Facing Dog

- Chair

- Child

Transitions: Encourage seamless transitions, allowing practitioners to melt into each pose with grace.

Breathwork coaching: Guide practitioners to breathe mindfully, savoring the quiet beauty of each breath.

Closing script: "As you conclude this dance of stillness, may the serenity of winter linger within you. In the silence, find the wisdom that whispers through the snowflakes."

Rest and Rejuvenate: A Symphony of Replenishment

Music: resonating at 963Hz, 396Hz, 432Hz, or 528Hz to stimulate all the chakras.

Opening script: "As we flow through these poses, may you embrace the profound truth that rest is an art, and it is just as productive as working."

Poses to consider:

- Happy Baby

- Child

- Cat-Cow

- Spinal Twist

- Thread the Needle

- Tree

Transitions: Encourage gentle transitions, allowing the body to surrender into each restorative pose.

Breathwork coaching: Guide practitioners to breathe deeply, inviting a sense of rejuvenation with each breath.

Closing script: "As you conclude this symphony of replenishment, may the rest you've gifted yourself be a source of vitality throughout winter's peaceful nights."

Surrender: Trusting the Universe's Grace

Music: resonating at 528Hz or 639Hz.

Opening script: "In the tender surrender to the universe, let us release the illusion of control. As we navigate through these poses, may you learn to trust, letting go of resistance and embracing the flow of life."

Poses to consider:

- Puppy

- Child's

- Side Plank

- Extended Side Angle

- Standing Forward Bend

- Lizard

Transitions: Encourage fluid transitions, embodying the ease of surrender.

Breathwork coaching: Guide practitioners to breathe with surrender, allowing each breath to be a bridge to trust and release.

Closing script: "As you conclude this practice of surrender, may the winter winds carry away any lingering burdens. In trust, find the freedom that comes with letting go."

New Beginnings: Embracing Change

Music: resonating at 528Hz or 639Hz for the solar plexus and heart chakras.

Opening script: "In the canvas of winter, let us welcome change with open arms. As we flow through these poses, may each movement signify a step towards new beginnings and the excitement of untapped opportunities."

Poses to consider:

- Sun Salutations

- Fierce

- Sunbird

- Downward Dog and Variations

- Lunge and Twists

- Firelog

Transitions: Encourage dynamic transitions, symbolizing the energy of new beginnings.

Breathwork coaching: Guide practitioners to breathe with anticipation, inhaling the freshness of change and exhaling any lingering resistance.

Closing script: "As you conclude this journey of new beginnings, may winter's embrace be a canvas for the vibrant brushstrokes of change. Embrace each moment with enthusiasm and an open heart.

Focus Inward: Introspection and Control

Music: resonating at 852Hz for the third eye chakra.

Opening script: "As we explore these poses, may you find strength in focusing on what you can control, acknowledging the power within."

Poses to consider:

- Butterfly

- Child

- Seated Forward Bend

- Head-to-Knee Forward Bend

- Camel

- Lotus

Transitions: Encourage deliberate transitions, connecting each pose with purpose.

Breathwork coaching: Guide practitioners to breathe with intention, drawing attention to the rhythm of self-discovery.

Closing script: "As you conclude this journey of introspection, may the winter stillness guide your focus inward."

Open Your Heart: Radiate Love and Acceptance

Music: resonating at 639Hz for the heart chakra.

Opening script: "As we gracefully move through these poses, may love flow freely within, and may you accept, feel, and spread love to all."

Poses to consider:

- Camel

- Sphinx

- Child

- Downward Facing Dog

- Bridge

- Cow

Transitions: Encourage heart-opening transitions, allowing the breath to guide each movement.

Breathwork coaching: Guide practitioners to breathe deeply, inviting love into every cell of their being.

Closing script: "As you conclude this practice of heart-opening, may the love within you be a beacon in the winter darkness. Radiate love, accept love, and be a vessel of warmth and compassion."

Connecting to Your Root Chakra: Grounding and Stability

Music: resonating at 396Hz for the root chakra

Opening script: "In the roots of grounding, let us find stability within. As we traverse through these poses, may you connect with the essence of your root chakra, anchoring yourself in inner stability."

Poses to consider:

- Garland

- Child

- Tree

- Lotus

- Warrior 2

- Crescent Moon

Transitions: Encourage grounding transitions, embodying the strength and stability of the rooted self.

Breathwork coaching: Guide practitioners to breathe with a sense of grounding, allowing each breath to sink roots into the earth.

Closing script: "As you conclude this exploration of grounding, may the roots you've planted within yourself provide the stability needed to weather the winter storms. In the strength of your roots, find your grounding."

Explore Your Shadows: A Journey Within

Music: resonating with 639Hz, 852Hz, and 963Hz for the heart, third eye and crown chakras.

Opening script: "As we navigate through these poses, may you recognize wounds and areas that deserve extra love."

Poses to consider:

- Upward Facing Dog

- Goddess Pose with Eagle Arms

- Upward Forward Fold with Hands on Shins

- Upward Extended Feet Pose with Arms Overhead and Thumbs Locked

- Garland

- Chair

Transitions: Encourage mindful transitions, allowing practitioners to explore their shadows with grace.

Breathwork coaching: Guide practitioners to breathe compassionately, acknowledging the areas that need a little extra love.

Closing script: "As you conclude this exploration of shadows, may you find beauty in acknowledging your wounds. "

Embrace Your Divine Feminine: Nurturing Grace

Music: resonating at 432Hz and 963Hz for the heart and crown chakras

Opening script: "In the essence of the Divine Feminine, let us embrace the nurturing grace within. As we gracefully move through these poses, may you connect with the beauty of the Divine Feminine dwelling inside you."

Poses to consider:
- High Lunge

- Garland

- One-Legged Pigeon

- Bow

- Child

- Shoulder Stand

Transitions: Encourage gentle transitions, allowing practitioners to embody the grace of the Divine Feminine.

Breathwork coaching: Guide practitioners to breathe with softness, inviting a sense of nurturing and acceptance.

Closing script: "As you conclude this journey into the Divine Feminine, may you carry the gentleness and nurturing energy within. In the embrace of your own grace, find peace and harmony."

New Hopes and Ideas: A Winter's Awakening

Music: resonating at 417Hz and 528Hz for the sacral and solar plexus chakras.

Opening script: "In the hush of winter, let us welcome new hopes and ideas. As we flow through these poses, may you embrace the possibilities that winter brings, cultivating excitement for new beginnings."

Poses to consider:
- Krishna

- Thunderbolt

- Downward Facing Dog

- Low Lunge

- Revolved Low Lunge

- Revolved High Lunge

Transitions: Encourage fluid transitions, symbolizing the flow of new energy and ideas.

Breathwork coaching: Guide practitioners to breathe with anticipation, inhaling the freshness of change and exhaling any lingering resistance.

Closing script: "As you conclude this journey of winter's awakening, may the cold winds carry away any doubts. Embrace the warmth of new beginnings and step into the light of possibility."

Compassion for Others: A Heartfelt Connection

Music: resonating at 639Hz for the heart chakra.

Opening script: "In the vibration of love, let us extend our hearts to others. As we navigate through these poses, may you open yourself to the boundless power of compassion, sharing warmth and human connection."

Poses to consider:
- Extended Puppy

- Sphinx

- Warrior 2

- Camel

- Corpse

- Bow

Transitions: Encourage heart-opening transitions, allowing practitioners to embody the expansive nature of compassion.

Breathwork coaching: Guide practitioners to breathe with love, inhaling compassion for oneself and exhaling love for others.

Closing script: "As you conclude this practice of compassion, may your heart remain open, and your spirit be a source of love."

Prioritize Your Needs: Self-Love Manifesto

Music: resonating at 396Hz for the root chakra.

Opening script: "In the sanctuary of self-love, let us prioritize our needs. As we gracefully move through these poses, may you show up for yourself first, honoring the sacred vessel that carries your spirit."

Poses to consider:

- Triangle

- Downward Facing Dog

- Tree

- Firefly

- Cobra

- Seated Forward Fold with Bound Half Lotus

Transitions: Encourage deliberate transitions, symbolizing the intentional act of prioritizing self-love.

Breathwork coaching: Guide practitioners to breathe with self-compassion, inhaling nurturing energy and exhaling any self-doubt.

Closing script: "As you conclude this journey of self-love, may your cup overflow with the love you've cultivated within. In the embrace of self-prioritization, find strength and resilience."

Feel Your Body's Strength: Power Within

Music: resonating at 396Hz, 528Hz, and 963Hz for the root, solar plexus, and crown chakras.

Opening script: "In the resonance of inner power, let us feel the strength within. As we navigate through these poses, may you recognize the immense power that resides in the very core of your being."

Poses to consider:

- Chair

- Crescent Lunge

- Plank

- Upward facing dog

- Warrior 2

- Bridge

Transitions: Encourage strong and intentional transitions, embodying the power inherent in each movement.

Breathwork coaching: Guide practitioners to breathe with strength, inhaling the power within and exhaling any sense of limitation.

Closing script: "As you conclude this journey into your inner strength, may you carry the awareness of your power. In the reservoir of your own strength, find confidence and resilience."

Connecting to Your Crown Chakra: Oneness of Being

Music: resonating at 963Hz for the crown chakra.

Opening script: "In the vibrations of unity, let us connect to the oneness of everything. As we gracefully move through these poses, may you attune your spirit to the divine frequency that unites us all."

Poses to consider:

- Lotus

- Tree

- Mountain

- Downward Dog

- Butterfly

- Rabbit

Transitions: Encourage fluid and gentle transitions, symbolizing the interconnectedness of all things.

Breathwork coaching: Guide practitioners to breathe with awareness, inhaling the universal energy and exhaling any sense of separation.

Closing script: "As you conclude this journey of unity, may you carry the essence of oneness within."

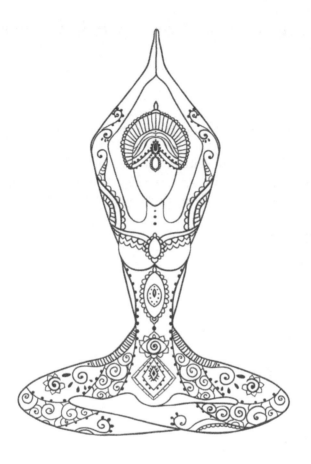

As the winter winds begin to wane, carrying with them the wisdom of introspection, we turn our gaze towards the promise of a new season. Spring, with its gentle blossoms and the dance of life returning to the earth, calls for a different kind of awakening. In the next chapter, we'll explore themes that mirror the vibrant energy of spring—renewal, growth, and the infinite possibilities that come with the thawing of winter's embrace. Join me as we unfold the mat, inviting the spirit of spring to guide us through practices that celebrate the awakening of life and the vibrant hues of a new beginning.

Chapter 5:

Spring

Within these pages, you will discover a collection of 27 carefully curated themes, each inspired by the invigorating energy of spring. From the blossoming of flowers to the revitalization of the earth, each theme captures the essence of this season's renewal. But this isn't just about words on a page; it's about bringing these themes to life in your yoga classes.

Starting New: Embracing Change and Welcoming New Opportunities

Music: Mix inspirational tunes with sounds of nature, like birdsong or gentle rainfall. Set the tone to 528Hz/639Hz frequencies.

Opening script: "Today, as we embrace change and welcome new opportunities, let the energy of spring guide us in this transformative journey on the mat."

Poses to consider:

- Downward Dog

- Happy Baby

- Child

- Standing Forward Bend

- Low Lunge

- Cobra

Transitions: Flow seamlessly, matching the rhythm of your breath.

Breathwork coaching: Inhale possibilities, exhale hesitation. Let your breath guide you into the uncharted territory of your potential.

Closing script: "As we open up to change, inviting new beginnings into our lives, may the seeds planted during this practice blossom in our hearts, creating endless possibilities."

Growth: Finding Strength in Adaptation

Music: Infuse the music with rhythmic Latin beats or soothing flutes to evoke the vibrant and creative energy associated with various cultures at 396Hz, 528Hz, or 639Hz frequencies.

Opening script: "In growth, we find our strength to adapt and welcome new opportunities. As we embark on a journey of growth, may this practice become a fertile ground for personal evolution and inner strength."

Poses to consider:

- Standing Forward Bend

- Cobra

- Mountain Tree

- Sun Salutation

- Extended Triangle

- Shoulder Stand

Transitions: Move gracefully, syncing breath with movement.

Breathwork coaching: Amid growth, let your breath nurture like rain. Inhale strength, exhale into poses. Connect with your breath, expanding into realms of personal growth.

Closing script: "With every pose, with every breath, feel the growth within, connecting to the world around and within ourselves."

Connecting to Your Sacral Chakra: Nurturing Feminine Energy and Creativity

Music: Align with the sacral chakra using 417Hz frequency. You can use Latin beats to create an energetic environment.

Opening script: "As we dive into the vibrant energy of the sacral chakra, let's connect with our feminine energy, creativity, and the life force pulsating within us."

Poses to consider:

- Goddess

- Low Lunge

- Half Monkey

- Warrior 2

- Reverse Warrior

- Wide-Legged Forward Bend

Transitions: Flow smoothly, nurturing the sacral energy.

Breathwork coaching: Center in the sacral chakra. Inhale feminine power, exhale blockages. Let breath dance with creativity, connecting with the life force within.

Closing script: "As you leave this practice, carry the grace of your sacral energy, igniting your creative flame and life force in every step."

Embrace New Beginnings: Accepting Change With Excitement

Music: Resonate with the solar plexus at 528Hz. Incorporate energetic tunes with a mix of cultural instruments.

Opening script: "As we resonate with the solar plexus, let's embrace new beginnings and step into the excitement of positive transformations awaiting us."

Poses to consider:

- Windmills

- Side Stretches

- Seated Twist

- Cat-Cow

- Forward Bend

- Downward Dog

Transitions: Transition mindfully, syncing breath and movement.

Breathwork coaching: With a focus on new beginnings, let your breath be the wind of change. Inhale acceptance, exhale resistance. Synchronize breath with acceptance and embrace possibilities.

Closing script: "In embracing new beginnings, may our hearts open to endless possibilities, and the energy of change propel us toward a brighter future."

Radiating Love: Giving Unconditional Love to Yourself and Others

Music: Use calming tracks with gentle Latin guitar or cultural flutes to create a nurturing and loving atmosphere. Elevate the heart chakra with 639Hz frequency.

Opening script: "As we elevate the heart chakra, let the practice become a sanctuary where unconditional love flows freely, embracing ourselves and radiating it to the world."

Poses to consider:

- Cobra

- Heart Melting

- Bridge

- Upward Bow

- Camel

- Wheel

Transitions: Move gracefully, letting love flow through your practice.

Breathwork coaching: Let your breath radiate love from the heart chakra. Inhale unconditional love, exhale, sharing it. Feel your heart opening, weaving compassion with each breath.

Closing script: "Radiate love to the world; let your heart be a beacon of compassion, carrying the warmth of this practice into your daily interactions."

Bloom When You Are Ready: Blossoming at Your Own Pace

Music: Combine 528Hz for the solar plexus and 741Hz for the throat chakra.

Opening script: "Combining energies for the solar plexus and throat chakra, let's take this practice as an opportunity to bloom at our own pace, recognizing the artistry within."

Poses to consider:

- Child

- Downward Facing Dog

- Low Lunge

- Upward Facing Dog

- Extended Triangle

- High Lunge

Transitions: Flow with intention, allowing yourself to bloom in your own time.

Breathwork coaching: Inhale patience, exhale urgency. Blossom at your pace with each mindful breath.

Closing script: "Blossom in your own time, for you are a work of art in progress, leaving the mat with the beauty of your unfolding journey."

Rise with the Sun: Embracing Your Natural Body and Letting the Sun Guide You

Music: Energize with 396Hz and 417Hz or uplifting morning tunes.

Opening script: "As we attune ourselves to the energizing frequencies, let this practice be a celebration of our natural bodies, rising with the sun's guidance."

Poses to consider:

- Sun Salutation

- Upward Salute

- Mountain

- Standing Forward Bend

- Low Lunge

- Plank

Transitions: Move dynamically, syncing breath with the rhythm of the day.

Breathwork coaching: Inhale possibilities, exhale shadows. Let your breath be sunlight, guiding you with renewed purpose.

Closing script: "With each sunrise, feel the warmth of new possibilities, carrying the vitality of the sun within as you step off the mat."

Honor the Earth: Rooting Yourself in the Earth and Honoring Its Strength Within You

Music: Feel yourself with 396Hz for the root chakra or grounding tunes.

Opening script: "In grounding ourselves with the frequency of the root chakra, let's connect to the Earth, acknowledging and honoring its strength within us."

Poses to consider:

- Downward Dog

- Child's Pose

- Mountain

- Standing Forward Bend

- Warrior 2

- Triangle

Transitions: Move mindfully, feeling the Earth's support.

Breathwork coaching: Inhale stability, exhale tension. Let your breath connect with the Earth's strength through mindful transitions.

Closing script: "Connected to the Earth, may we carry the grounding strength of our roots into our daily lives, stepping forward with resilience and stability."

Planting Seeds: Welcoming Change and New Beginnings as You Plant Seeds of Intention

Music: Set the foundation with 396Hz for the root. Combine cultural sounds like Indian sitar or bamboo flutes with calming instrumental tracks for a meditative experience.

Opening script: "As we establish a foundation with the root frequency, let's embrace the energy of change and intentionally plant seeds that will grow into the garden of our aspirations."

Poses to consider:

- Seated and Sleeping Swan

- Half Shoelace

- Full Shoelace

- Dragonfly

- Fire Log

- Mountain

Transitions: Flow with purpose, nurturing the seeds within.

Breathwork coaching: As you plant intention seeds, let breath be nourishing soil. Inhale aspirations, exhale grounding. Synchronize breath with purpose, infusing life into intentions.

Closing script: "In each pose, nurture the seeds within, cultivating the garden of your intentions, ready to blossom in the seasons to come."

Spring Cleaning: Letting Go of the Old and Making Room for the New

Music: Cleanse with 417Hz and 639Hz frequencies. Use music with flutes to emphasize the theme of letting go and creating space.

Opening script: "As the cleansing frequencies envelop us, let go of the old with each breath, creating space for the freshness of new beginnings to flow into your life."

Poses to consider:

- Seated Spinal Twist

- Eagle

- Downward Facing Dog

- Standing Forward Fold

- Knees to Chest

- Revolved Triangle

Transitions: Transition with release, shedding the old with each breath.

Breathwork coaching: Cleanse for new beginnings with breath as a purifying force. Inhale freshness, exhale stagnant energy. Let breath sweep away the old, creating room for vibrant energy.

Closing script: "With every exhale, release what no longer serves; inhale the revitalizing energy of this practice, stepping into a renewed chapter."

Honor Your Divine Feminine: Honoring Your Divine Feminine and Embracing the Creative Energy Within

Music: Connect with the sacral chakra using the gentle vibrations of 417Hz. Integrate world music with a focus on feminine rhythms and melodies, such as Middle Eastern instruments or soothing vocal chants.

Opening script: "With the gentle vibrations of the sacral chakra, let's honor the Divine Feminine, embracing the creative energy that flows gracefully within us."

Poses to consider:

- High Lunge

- Garland

- One-Legged Pigeon

- Child's Pose

- Shoulder Stand

- Bow

Transitions: Move gracefully, honoring the flow of feminine energy.

Breathwork coaching: Connect with sacred feminine energy through breath. Inhale goddess strength, exhale imbalance. Let breath be the dance of divine feminine energy, guiding transitions.

Closing script: "As you leave the mat, carry the grace of your Divine Feminine in every step, embodying the strength and beauty of this sacred energy."

Make Room for Change: Making Space for New Beginnings and Opportunities

Music: Blend frequencies of 396Hz, 417Hz, 528Hz, and 639Hz to welcome change. Combine diverse music genres like African drums or Latin percussion with modern beats.

Opening script: "Blending frequencies, we embark on a journey of change, creating space within ourselves for the endless possibilities that new beginnings bring."

Poses to consider:
- Cobra and Variations

- Downward Facing Dog

- Locust

- Revolved Low Lunge

- Hero

- Triangle

Transitions: Flow smoothly, accepting change with each breath.

Breathwork coaching: Let breath be the wind of change. Inhale possibilities, exhale surrender. Sync breath with acceptance, feeling openness in each breath.

Closing script: "May this practice open doors to the limitless opportunities that change unfolds, guiding us with each breath into a future filled with possibilities."

Find Inspiration: Tapping Into Your Creative Energy and Letting Inspiration Guide Your Practice

Music: Awaken your sacral chakra with the harmonious sounds of 417Hz. Add diverse instrumental tracks like Indian sitar, or Native American flutes.

Opening script: "As the harmonious sounds resonate within, connect with the sacral chakra and allow the river of inspiration to flow through your practice."

Poses to consider:
- Krishna
- Warrior 1
- Warrior 2
- Downward Facing Dog
- Low Lunge Variations

- Revolved High Lunge

Transitions: Move with the rhythm of your creative spirit.

Breathwork coaching: Tap into inspiration within through breath. Inhale creativity, exhale blocks. Allow breath to be the current of inspiration, shaping your journey.

Closing script: "Inspiration is a river that flows within; let it guide your journey beyond the mat, infusing creativity into every aspect of your life."

Birth Creativity: Bringing Creativity Into Every Movement and Every Breath

Music: Set the sacral chakra's frequency at 417Hz. Blend cultural sounds like South American pan flutes or ethnic percussion.

Opening script: "With the sacral chakra as our guide, let's embark on a practice where every pose, every breath, becomes a canvas for the expression of our creative spark."

Poses to consider:
- Warrior 1

- Downward Facing Dog

- Half Moon

- Lunge Variations

- Goddess

- Crow

Transitions: Flow with the intention of nurturing your creative spark.

Breathwork coaching: Let breath be the life force birthing creativity. Inhale imagination, exhale manifestation. Sync breath with nurturing your creative spark.

Closing script: "As you leave your mat, carry the seeds of creativity you've planted within, nurturing them into the blossoming artistry of your daily life."

Inner Goddess: Tapping Into Your Feminine Power

Music: Resonate with 417Hz or elevate to 639Hz for a profound connection. Integrate empowering and rhythmic tracks with elements like Latin beats or tribal drums.

Opening script: "As the resonance surrounds us, let's delve into a practice that honors the divine feminine within, connecting with the strength and grace of our inner goddess."

Poses to consider:
- High Lunge

- Garland

- Child's Pose

- Shoulder Stand

- Warrior 2

- Camel

Transitions: Move with the grace and power of your inner goddess.

Breathwork coaching: Connect with the divine feminine through breath. Inhale inner goddess strength, exhale self-doubt. Let breath be the dance of grace and power, empowering each movement.

Closing script: "In every pose, may you feel the power and beauty of your divine feminine energy, carrying its essence as a guiding light beyond the practice."

Re-energize: Energizing Yourself From Within and Feeling the Renewal in Every Breath

Music: Revitalize with the frequency of 528Hz. Use uplifting cultural rhythms.

Opening script: "As the revitalizing frequency surrounds us, let this practice be a journey of self-energizing renewal, feeling the vitality in each breath and movement."

Poses to consider:

- Downward Facing Dog

- Cobra

- Low Lunge

- Tree

- Forward Fold

- Warrior 1

Transitions: Move dynamically, syncing breath with revitalization.

Breathwork coaching: Revitalize within through breath. Inhale renewal, exhale release. Feel the energy of creation in every breath, carrying renewed vitality beyond your mat.

Closing script: "Carry this renewed energy with you as you step back into the world, radiating the vibrancy of your revitalized self."

Aliven the Senses: Awakening the Senses With Each Pose

Music: Uplift with any frequency that feels invigorating. Combine invigorating tracks with diverse cultural instruments, such as African drums or traditional flutes.

Opening script: "As we uplift our spirits, let's explore the poses with a heightened sense of aliveness, awakening our senses to the richness of the present moment."

Poses to consider:

- Sun Salutation

- High Lunge

- Warrior 3

- Standing Split

- Staff

- High Lunge Twist

Transitions: Move mindfully, awakening the senses with each pose.

Breathwork coaching: Awaken your senses with the breath as your guide. Inhale aliveness, exhale stagnation. Let each breath be a mindful journey, reawakening your senses.

Closing script: "As you reawaken your senses, carry this heightened aliveness into your daily life, savoring each moment as a celebration of being fully alive."

Sun Salutations: Connecting With the Sun, Source of Light and Energy

Music: Harmonize with the heart chakra frequency at 639Hz. Infuse the music with bright and uplifting sounds, including Latin guitar or Caribbean steel drums.

Opening script: "In harmonizing with the heart chakra, let this practice be a celebration of our connection with the sun, drawing upon its light and energy in each movement."

Poses to consider:

- Sun Salutations

- Downward Dog

- Mountain

- Forward Fold

- Cobra

- Plank

Transitions: Flow with the grace and warmth of the sun.

Breathwork coaching: Harmonize with the sun's energy through breath. Inhale light, exhale shadows. Allow breath to be the rhythm of your salutations, connecting with the warmth within.

Closing Script: "As the sun shines within, carry its light into the world, spreading warmth and positivity wherever your journey takes you."

Clear Out the Old: Letting Go of Clutter and Making Room for What Serves You

Music: Cleanse with frequencies of 417Hz, 639Hz, or 741Hz. Use diverse sounds, such as Asian bamboo flutes or Native American drums.

Opening script: "As we cleanse with these frequencies, release the clutter within and around, creating a sacred space that invites in what truly serves your highest self."

Poses to consider:

- Downward Dog

- Child Pose

- Forward Fold

- Cobra

- Reclined Twist

- Cat-Cow

Transitions: Transition with release, shedding the old with each breath.

Breathwork coaching: Cleansing breath to release the old. Inhale freshness, exhale stagnation. Let breath be the cleansing wave, clearing space for the new to unfold.

Closing script: "With each exhale, release what no longer serves; inhale the freshness of new beginnings, embracing the clarity that comes with letting go."

Be Kind to Yourself: Showering Yourself With Love and Care

Music: Nurture with the heart's frequency at 639Hz. Integrate nurturing tunes with elements like acoustic guitar or gentle Latin rhythms.

Opening script: "With the nurturing frequency of the heart, let this practice be a gentle shower of love and care upon yourself, cultivating a deep sense of self-kindness."

Poses to consider:

- Camel

- Humble Warrior

- Upward Facing Dog

- Triangle

- Bow

- Sphinx

Transitions: Move with gentleness, honoring your body and spirit.

Breathwork coaching: Nurture yourself through breath. Inhale self-love, exhale doubt. Let breath be a gentle embrace, showering kindness upon your being.

Closing script: "As you leave your mat, carry the kindness you've given yourself into the world, radiating compassion and gentleness in every interaction."

Celebrate the Spring Equinox: Connecting With the Vibrant Energy of Springtime

Music: Harmonize with the sacral chakra's frequency, 417Hz. Use sounds such as Celtic melodies.

Opening script: "Harmonizing with the sacral chakra, let's celebrate the spring equinox, immersing ourselves in the revitalizing energy that marks the arrival of spring."

Poses to consider:

- Dynamic Chair

- Cactus Crescent Lunge

- Wide-Legged Forward Bend

- High Lunge

- Warrior 3

- Twisted Chair

Transitions: Flow with the essence of renewal, mirroring the changing seasons.

Breathwork coaching: Inhale the essence of the equinox, exhale into renewal. Let breath mirror the changing seasons, celebrating the vibrant energy of spring.

Closing script: "As you step off the mat, carry the revitalizing spirit of the equinox within, embracing the blossoming transformations that come with each season."

Inner Power: Ignite It and Embrace the Strength Within

Music: Ignite your solar plexus with the empowering frequency of 528Hz. Use rhythmic sounds like African drums or Middle Eastern instruments.

Opening script: "With the empowering frequency resonating, let's ignite the flame of our inner power, embodying the strength and confidence that reside within us."

Poses to consider:

- Warrior 1

- Warrior 2

- Warrior 3

- Forearm Plank.

- Chair

- Tree

Transitions: Move with purpose, embodying the strength of your inner power.

Breathwork coaching: Ignite your inner power through breath. Inhale strength, exhale limitations. Sync breath with purpose, embodying the flame of your inner power.

Closing script: "May the flame of your inner power guide you in every step, empowering you to navigate life with courage and authenticity."

Breath of Life: Finding the Essence of Life Force Energy in the Breath

Music: Connect with the root, sacral, throat, and crown chakras using frequencies 396Hz, 417Hz, 741Hz, or 963Hz. Blend diverse instrumental tracks representing various cultures, incorporating instruments like didgeridoo, sitar or flutes.

Opening script: "As we connect with various chakras through frequencies, let the breath be the thread weaving through them, connecting us to the essence of life force energy."

Poses to consider:

- Child

- Forward Bend

- Twist

- Mountain

- Standing Spinal Roll Up

- Downward Facing Dog

Transitions: Flow with the rhythm of your breath, the source of life.

Breathwork coaching: Connect with the essence of life force through breath. Inhale vitality, exhale stagnation. Let breath be the rhythmic flow of life within every pose.

Closing script: "As you breathe, feel the vitality of life pulsating through your entire being, anchoring you in the present moment and the interconnectedness of all life."

Connecting to Your Solar Plexus Chakra: The Power Within

Music: Tune into the solar plexus with the frequency of 528Hz. Infuse the music with empowering sounds, including Latin rhythms.

Opening script: "Tuning into the solar plexus, let this practice be a journey of connecting with the power residing within, embracing the courage and personal strength anchored there."

Poses to consider:

- Bow

- Mountain

- Cobra

- Downward Facing Dog

- Crescent Moon

- Bridge

Transitions: Move with intention, linking each pose to the energy center.

Breathwork coaching: Empower your solar plexus through breath. Inhale personal strength, exhale doubt. Let breath guide each movement, connecting with your inner source of power.

Closing script: "May the power of your solar plexus guide you in every decision, leading you towards a path of authenticity and personal empowerment."

Be Present: Embracing the Importance of Living in the Now

Music: Elevate your solar plexus with the resonant frequency of 528Hz. Use grounding frequencies along with cultural sounds, such as traditional Asian instruments.

Opening script: "With the resonant frequency elevating our solar plexus, let's immerse ourselves in the present moment, acknowledging the importance of living fully in the now."

Poses to consider:

- Mountain

- Triangle

- Warrior 1

- Warrior 2

- Pigeon

- Staff

Transitions: Flow mindfully, grounding yourself in the present.

Breathwork coaching: Ground yourself in the present through breath. Inhale the now, exhale distractions. Let breath be your anchor, grounding you in the beauty of each moment.

Closing script: "As you leave this practice, carry the gift of presence into your day, savoring each moment as a precious opportunity for growth and joy."

Celebrate the Small Things: Expressing Gratitude

Music: Connect with the heart chakra at 617Hz. Integrate uplifting tunes with elements like Latin guitar or cultural flutes.

Opening script: "Harmonizing with the heart chakra, let's weave gratitude into every pose, celebrating the small things that add richness to the tapestry of our lives."

Poses to consider:

- Camel

- Seated Forward Fold

- Mountain

- Forward Fold

- Knees to Chest

- Low Lunge

Transitions: Move with gratitude, savoring each pose as a celebration.

Breathwork coaching: Gratitude in each breath. Inhale joy, exhale gratitude. Allow your breath to cherish the beauty found in every small detail.

Closing script: "May your heart overflow with gratitude for the beauty in the small things, and may this practice inspire a continuous celebration of life's simple joys."

Choose Joy: Your Guiding Light

Music: Elevate the heart chakra with the uplifting frequency of 617Hz. Use diverse sounds, such as the Caribbean steel drums or African rhythms.

Opening script: "Uplifting the heart chakra, let each breath be a conscious choice to embrace joy, allowing it to guide our movements and infuse our practice with lightness."

Poses to consider:
- Cat-Cow

- Low Lunge

- High Crescent Lunge

- Tree

- Sun Salutation

- Gate

Transitions: Flow with joy, allowing each movement to express your happiness.

Breathwork coaching: Choose joy with each breath. Inhale happiness, exhale negativity. Let breath be the melody of joy, guiding you through the dance of life.

Closing script: "As you step off the mat, carry the choice of joy into your journey, radiating positivity and choosing happiness in every moment."

The energy of spring has laid the foundation for growth, and now we transition to a chapter that celebrates the sun-kissed days and the vitality of summer. In the next chapter, we'll dive into 27 themes curated to embrace the radiance of the sun, fostering strength, flexibility, and a sense of lightness. So, let the warmth of spring guide us into the vibrant embrace of summer, where the yoga journey continues under the sun's golden glow.

Chapter 6:

Summer

Summer, with its radiant energy, provides a canvas for self-expression and empowerment. Each theme presented in this chapter is designed to align with the unique qualities of this season, encouraging both yoga practitioners and teachers to embrace the transformative power of the sun's glow. Whether you're looking to deepen your personal practice or infuse your teaching with creativity, these themes offer a holistic approach to well-being that encompasses physical, mental, and emotional dimensions.

Feel Freedom: Embracing Liberation and Unleashing Your True Self

Music: Let it resonate with the frequencies of liberation—396Hz, 417Hz, or 528Hz.

Opening script: "As we step into the dance of life, find freedom in every breath. Let each movement be a celebration of liberation."

Poses to consider:

- Low Lunge

- Goddess

- Extended Triangle

- Half Moon

- Half Moon Bow

- Monkey

Transitions: Flow seamlessly, like a gentle breeze moving through each pose. Inhale, exhale, and let your breath guide you.

Breathwork coaching: Inhale deeply, absorbing the essence of freedom. Exhale, releasing any tension. Feel the expansion with each breath, letting freedom permeate every cell.

Closing script: "As the dance concludes, carry the essence of freedom with you. May each step outside the mat be a continued celebration of liberation."

Embrace Non-Attachment: Welcoming Detachment and Finding Freedom in Letting Go

Music: Let the music be at 396Hz, 417Hz, or 528Hz for the root, sacral and solar chakras. You can also incorporate sounds from African drums or Middle Eastern instruments.

Opening script: "Release attachments and discover the lightness within. In the dance of letting go, find the beauty of your being."

Poses to consider:

- Chair

- Easy Pose

- Cat-Cow

- Downward Facing Dog

- Pigeon

- Triangle

Transitions: Flow gracefully from one pose to the next, embracing the fluidity of letting go.

Breathwork coaching: Inhale the present moment, exhale attachments. Feel the lightness within, cultivating space for new beginnings.

Closing script: "As you step away from the practice, carry the beauty of non-attachment within. Embrace the lightness that comes from releasing what no longer serves you."

Find Stillness: Cultivating Calmness and Discovering Serenity Within

Music: Set the tone at 396Hz or 417Hz for the root and solar chakras. Infuse them with calming melodies inspired by Asian traditional instruments like the bamboo flute or Japanese koto.

Opening script: "In the embrace of stillness, discover the power of presence. Let each pose be a journey into the calm energy within."

Poses to consider:

- Mountain

- Chair

- Standing Forward Bend

- Low Lunge

- High Lunge

- Revolved Lunge

Transitions: Move mindfully, transitioning with purpose and intention.

Breathwork coaching: Inhale the stillness, exhale distractions. Feel the calm energy within, allowing it to permeate your practice.

Closing script: "As you move beyond the stillness of the practice, carry the power of presence with you. May each moment off the mat be guided by the calm energy you've cultivated."

Release Judgment: Letting Go of Judgment and Embracing Compassion

Music: Let the music be at 639Hz for the heart chakra. Incorporate diverse world music elements, exploring sounds from Latin America, the Caribbean, or indigenous instruments.

Opening script: "Release judgment and open your heart to boundless love. In the dance of self-kindness, find warmth flooding your being."

Poses to consider:

- Child

- Downward Facing Dog

- Warrior 1

- Plank

- Forearm Plank

- Sphinx

Transitions: Flow seamlessly, allowing each movement to be a gesture of self-kindness.

Breathwork coaching: Inhale love, exhale judgment. Feel the warmth of self-acceptance flooding your being.

Closing script: "As the practice concludes, carry the warmth of self-love. Let every step resonate with the release of judgment and the embrace of boundless love."

Connecting to Your Heart Chakra: Nurturing Love and Compassion in Your Heart Center

Music: Explore a fusion of Indian classical music with modern beats or incorporate elements from Native American flute music, aligning with the heart chakra's frequencies at 639Hz.

Opening script: "In the heart's embrace, connect to the love within and around you. Let the poses be a dance of love, and the transitions, gestures of self-acceptance."

Poses to consider:

- Camel

- Downward-Facing Dog.

- Sphinx

- Cobra

- Bow

- Triangle

Transitions: Flow gracefully, allowing each movement to be a dance of love.

Breathwork coaching: Inhale love, exhale gratitude. Feel the love within and let it radiate through your practice.

Closing script: "As you leave the mat, let the dance of love continue. Carry the connection to your heart chakra, allowing love to radiate through every aspect of your being."

Let Love in: Opening Your Heart to Receive and Share Love

Music: Infuse the practice with soulful R&B, gospel, or jazz tunes, resonating with the heart chakra frequencies at 639Hz.

Opening script: "In openness, invite the abundance of love into your life. Let each pose and transition be a dance of openness."

Poses to consider:

- Downward-Facing Dog

- Camel

- Cow

- Upward-Facing Dog

- 8 Point

- Cobra

Transitions: Flow gracefully, letting each transition be a dance of openness.

Breathwork coaching: Inhale love, exhale resistance. Feel the abundant love within and allow it to permeate your entire being.

Closing script: "As the practice concludes, carry the dance of openness with you. Inhale love, exhale resistance, and let abundant love permeate your entire being."

Quiet Your Mind: Calming the Mental Chatter and Cultivating Inner Silence

Music: Integrate ambient sounds, such as nature-inspired music or gentle electronic tones, set at 852Hz or 963Hz for the third eye and crown chakras.

Opening script: "In the stillness of your mind, find clarity and inner peace. Let each pose guide you into the serenity within, and each transition be a journey."

Poses to consider:

- Child's

- Cow

- Cat

- Downward-Facing Dog

- Standing Forward Bend

- Supine Spinal Twist

Transitions: Move mindfully, allowing each transition to be a journey into inner stillness.

Breathwork coaching: Inhale clarity, exhale mental chatter. Feel the serenity within, allowing it to permeate your practice.

Closing script: "As you step away, may the serenity within accompany you. Inhale clarity, exhale mental chatter, and let the stillness of your mind guide your path."

Empower Yourself: Strengthening Your Inner Power

Music: Bring in empowering sounds from different cultures, such as African drumming or Native American chants, resonating with frequencies at 417Hz or 528Hz.

Opening script: "In the center of your being, find the strength to empower yourself. Let each movement declare personal empowerment, and every breath be infused with strength."

Poses to consider:

- Plank Pose

- Extended Side Angle Pose

- Warrior 1

- Warrior 2

- Dolphin Pose

- Locust Pose

Transitions: Flow seamlessly, allowing each movement to be a declaration of personal empowerment.

Breathwork coaching: Inhale strength, exhale self-doubt. Feel the power within and let it radiate through your practice.

Closing script: "Carry the power within as you conclude the practice. Inhale strength, exhale self-doubt, and let the declaration of personal empowerment resonate in every aspect of your life."

Release Fear: Letting Go of Fear and Inviting Courage Into Your Life

Music: Explore uplifting sounds from diverse genres like reggae, calypso, or world fusion, set at 528Hz or 639Hz for the solar plexus and heart chakras.

Opening script: "In releasing fear, step into the light of courage. Let each pose and transition be a journey into fearlessness."

Poses to consider:

- Child

- Downward Facing Dog

- Standing Forward Bend

- Tree

- Mountain

- Easy

Transitions: Flow gracefully, allowing each transition to be a journey into fearlessness.

Breathwork coaching: Inhale courage, exhale fear. Feel the fearless energy within, empowering you to face any challenge.

Closing script: "As you step off the mat, let fearlessness guide you. Inhale courage, exhale fear, and feel the fearless energy empowering you to face any challenge."

Peel Back the Layers: Uncovering Your Authentic Self by Peeling Away External Influences

Music: Mix sounds from various cultural backgrounds, incorporating elements of traditional instruments or chants, set at 528Hz and 852Hz for the solar plexus and third eye chakras.

Opening script: "In peeling back the layers, uncover the truth of your authentic self. Let each movement reveal the radiant truth within."

Poses to consider:

- Restorative Child

- Goddess

- Plank

- Triangle

- Warrior 1

- Down Dog

Transitions: Flow seamlessly, allowing each movement to be a revelation of your authentic self.

Breathwork coaching: Inhale self-discovery, exhale self-doubt. Feel the layers peeling away, revealing the radiant truth of your being.

Closing script: "Carry the authenticity beyond the practice. Inhale self-discovery, exhale self-doubt, and feel the layers peeled away, exposing the beautiful truth of your being."

Say Yes to You: Affirming Yourself and Embracing Self-Approval

Music: Infuse uplifting tunes with a mix of Afrobeat, Caribbean rhythms, or Latin influences, resonating with the solar plexus at 528Hz.

Opening script: "In saying yes to yourself, find strength and balance. Let each pose and transition be a declaration of self-affirmation."

Poses to consider:

- Child

- Tree

- Cat-Cow

- Downward-Facing Dog

- Low Lunge

- Straight Leg Lunge

Transitions: Flow seamlessly, allowing each movement to be a declaration of self-affirmation.

Breathwork coaching: Inhale self-acceptance, exhale any self-doubt. Let each breath be a commitment to your well-being.

Closing script: "Conclude the practice with the echoes of self-affirmation. Inhale self-acceptance, exhale self-doubt, and let each breath be a commitment to your well-being."

Listen to Your Body: Tuning Into Your Body's Wisdom and Responding With Care

Music: Tune into the frequencies of 396Hz and 852Hz, grounding yourself in the root and third eye chakras.

Opening scripts: "As you listen to your body, discover the wisdom within. Let each pose and transition be a conversation with your own body."

Poses to consider:

- Child

- Downward Facing Dog

- Cat-Cow Pose

- Bridge Pose

- Spinal Twist

- Triangle

Transitions: Move mindfully, letting each transition be a conversation with your own body.

Breathwork coaching: Inhale awareness, exhale tension. Allow each breath to deepen your connection with your body's needs.

Closing script: "As you step away, carry the wisdom within. Inhale awareness, exhale tension, and let each breath deepen your connection with your body's needs."

Grounding: Anchoring Yourself in the Present Moment and Connecting With the Earth

Music: Integrate grounding sounds inspired by indigenous cultures or incorporate sounds of ocean waves and nature, set at 396Hz, grounding yourself in the root chakra.

Opening script: "In grounding into Earth, find stability and strength. Let each movement affirm your rooted presence and connection with the present moment."

Poses to consider:
- Downward Facing Dog

- Child

- Mountain

- Hero

- Easy Pose with a Twist.

- Warrior 2

Transitions: Flow with purpose, allowing each movement to be an affirmation of your rooted presence.

Breathwork coaching: Inhale stability, exhale uncertainty. Let each breath ground you in the present moment.

Closing script: "Carry the stability beyond the mat. Inhale stability, exhale uncertainty, and let each breath ground you in the beauty of the present moment."

Serve Yourself First: Prioritizing Self-Care and Nurturing Your Well-Being

Music: Elevate your practice with the harmonies of 528Hz and 639Hz, resonating with the solar plexus and heart.

Opening script: "In serving yourself first, create a foundation of strength and love. Let each pose and transition be an act of self-service."

Poses to consider:

- Tree

- Child

- Standing Forward Bend

- Goddess

- Mountain

- Cat-Cow

Transitions: Flow seamlessly, allowing each movement to be an act of self-service.

Breathwork coaching: Inhale self-love, exhale any sense of obligation. Let each breath be a reminder of your worthiness.

Closing script: "As you conclude, carry the foundation within. Inhale self-love, exhale any sense of obligation, and let each breath remind you of your worthiness."

Pursue Passion: Following Your Passions and Infusing Your Life With Purpose

Music: Energize your practice with the stimulating frequencies of 417Hz, resonating with the sacral chakra.

Opening script: "In pursuing your passion, embrace the vitality of your being. Let each movement be a celebration of your vibrant spirit."

Poses to consider:
- Standing Forward Fold

- Downward Dog

- Crescent Moon

- Butterfly

- Goddess

- Bow

Transitions: Flow with purpose, letting each movement be a dance of passion.

Breathwork coaching: Inhale creative energy, exhale any stagnation. Let each breath be a celebration of your vibrant spirit.

Closing script: "Conclude the practice with the celebration of passion. Inhale creative energy, exhale any stagnation, and let each breath be a celebration of your vibrant spirit."

Celebrate the Summer Solstice: Honoring the Peak of Summer

Music: Celebrate the longest day of the year with inspiring, lyricless music reminiscent of City of the Sun.

Opening script: "In the dance of light, celebrate the summer solstice and your own radiant potential. Let each pose and transition be a celebration of the sun's energy."

Poses to consider:
- Downward Dog

- Cobra

- Sun Salutations

- Standing Forward Fold

- Child

- Mountain

Transitions: Flow gracefully, allowing each movement to be a celebration of the sun's energy.

Breathwork coaching: Inhale light, exhale any darkness. Let each breath be a celebration of your own radiant potential.

Closing script: "As you step away, carry the celebration within. Inhale light, exhale any darkness, and let each breath be a celebration of your own radiant potential."

Accept What Is: Embracing the Present Moment and Accepting Life as It Comes

Music: Incorporate calming sounds inspired by Middle Eastern or Asian traditions, such as Sufi music or Tibetan singing bowls, set at 528Hz, resonating with the solar plexus

Opening script: "In accepting what is, find peace in the present moment. Let each pose and transition be a journey into acceptance."

Poses to consider:

- Corpse

- Legs Up the Wall

- Seated Forward Bend.

- Easy

- Fish

- Child

Transitions: Move with ease, allowing each transition to be a journey into acceptance.

Breathwork coaching: Inhale acceptance, exhale resistance. Let each breath guide you into a state of profound acceptance.

Closing script: "As you conclude, carry the peace within. Inhale acceptance, exhale resistance, and let each breath guide you into a state of profound acceptance."

Choose to Believe: Cultivating Belief in Yourself and Your Potential

Music: Elevate your practice with the harmonies of 639Hz and 852Hz, resonating with the heart and third eye chakras.

Opening script: "In choosing to believe, cultivate trust in the universe and your own journey. Let each movement be a testament to your choice to believe."

Poses to consider:

- Child

- Puppy

- Thread the Needle

- Warrior 1

- Plank

- Downward Dog

Transitions: Flow gracefully, allowing each movement to be a testament to your choice to believe.

Breathwork coaching: Inhale trust, exhale doubt. Let each breath strengthen your belief in the beauty of your journey.

Closing script: "As you step off the mat, carry the belief within. Inhale trust, exhale doubt, and let each breath strengthen your belief in the beauty of your journey."

Embrace Imperfections: Recognizing the Beauty in Imperfection

Music: Infuse your practice with the soothing frequencies of 528Hz or 639Hz, resonating with the heart and solar plexus chakras.

Opening script: "In embracing imperfections, honor the uniqueness of your being. Let each movement be a celebration of your unique journey."

Poses to consider:

- Lord of the Dance

- Bow

- Fire Log

- Child

- Eight-Angle

- Triangle

Transitions: Move mindfully, allowing each transition to be a celebration of your unique journey.

Breathwork coaching: Inhale self-love, exhale any judgment. Let each breath be a celebration of the imperfect, yet beautiful, you.

Closing script: "Conclude the practice with self-celebration. Inhale self-love, exhale any judgment, and let each breath be a celebration of the imperfect, yet beautiful, you."

Move to Meditate: Incorporating Movement into Meditation for a Mind-Body Connection

Music: Explore meditative sounds inspired by different cultures, such as traditional Japanese meditation music or sounds from the Himalayas. Elevate your practice with the transcendental frequencies of 963Hz, resonating with the crown chakra.

Opening script: "In moving to meditate, find stillness within the dance of life. Let each pose and transition guide you into a state of meditation."

Poses to consider:

- Child

- Downward Dog

- Lotus

- Cobra

- Butterfly

- Low Lunge

Transitions: Flow with purpose, letting each movement guide you into a state of meditation.

Breathwork coaching: Inhale stillness, exhale any restlessness. Let each breath be a gateway to the serenity within the dance of life.

Closing script: "As you conclude, carry the stillness within. Inhale stillness, exhale any restlessness, and let each breath be a gateway to the serenity within the dance of life."

Break Down Your Walls: Dissolving Emotional Barriers and Opening Yourself Up

Music: Immerse yourself in the harmonious tones of 639Hz, resonating with the heart chakra.

Opening script: "As you break down your walls, embrace vulnerability and radiate love into the world. Let each pose and transition symbolize the breaking down of emotional barriers."

Poses to consider:

- Child

- Camel

- Puppy

- Thread the Needle

- Cat-Cow

- Pigeon

Transitions: Flow seamlessly, allowing each movement to symbolize the breaking down of emotional barriers.

Breathwork coaching: Inhale love, exhale resistance. Let each breath dismantle the walls around your heart.

Closing script: "Step away with an open heart. Inhale love, exhale resistance, and let each breath dismantle the walls around your heart."

Connecting to Your Third Eye: Awakening Intuition and Tapping Into Inner Wisdom

Music: Integrate sounds that enhance introspection, such as traditional Indian ragas or ambient sounds inspired by mystical traditions, set at 852Hz for the third eye chakra.

Opening script: "In connecting to your third eye, embrace intuition and inner wisdom. Let each movement be a journey into the expansiveness of your third eye."

Poses to consider:

- Plow

- Downward Dog

- Lotus

- Child

- Legs Up the Wall

- Locust

Transitions: Flow gracefully, allowing each transition to be a journey into the expansiveness of your third eye.

Breathwork coaching: Inhale clarity, exhale illusion. Let each breath awaken your inner sight.

Closing script: "As you step off the mat, carry the inner wisdom within. Inhale clarity, exhale illusion, and let each breath awaken your inner sight."

Be Joyous: Cultivating Joy and Infusing Positivity Into Your Being

Music: Infuse your practice with the uplifting tones of 639Hz, resonating with the heart chakra.

Opening script: "Choose joy in every moment, celebrating the beauty of life. Let each pose and transition be a dance of joy."

Poses to consider:

- Camel

- Child

- Happy Baby

- Downward Dog

- Cat-Cow

- Dancer

Transitions: Move with lightness, allowing each transition to be a dance of joy.

Breathwork coaching: Inhale joy, exhale any heaviness. Let each breath be a celebration of the joyous spirit within.

Closing script: "As you conclude, carry the joy within. Inhale joy, exhale any heaviness, and let each breath be a celebration of the joyous spirit within."

Unconditional Love: Embracing Love Without Conditions, Both for Yourself and Others

Music: Explore sounds that evoke a sense of unity and compassion, incorporating elements from various cultural traditions, set at 639Hz, resonating with the heart chakra.

Opening script: "As a vessel of unconditional love, radiate compassion to yourself and others. Let each pose and transition be a journey into unconditional love."

Poses to consider:

- Bridge

- Camel

- Cobra

- Bow

- Sphinx

- Fish

Transitions: Move with compassion, allowing each transition to be a journey into unconditional love.

Breathwork coaching: Inhale love, exhale judgment. Let each breath be a manifestation of boundless, unconditional love.

Closing script: "Step away as a vessel of love. Inhale love, exhale judgment, and let each breath be a manifestation of boundless, unconditional love."

Explore Yourself: Delving Into Self-Exploration and Gaining Deeper Insights

Music: Embark on a journey of self-discovery with the introspective frequencies of 528Hz or 852Hz, resonating with the solar plexus and third eye chakras.

Opening script: "In exploring yourself, embrace the richness of your inner landscape. Let each movement be a step into self-exploration."

Poses to consider:

- Child

- Downward Dog

- Mountain

- Cat-Cow

- Downward Dog

- Corpse

Transitions: Move with mindfulness, allowing each transition to be a step into self-exploration.

Breathwork coaching: Inhale self-awareness, exhale self-judgment. Let each breath guide you into the richness of self-discovery.

Closing script: "Conclude the practice with self-awareness. Inhale self-awareness, exhale self-judgment, and let each breath guide you into the richness of self-discovery."

Embrace Your Inner Teenager: Connecting With the Playful and Adventurous Spirit Within

Music: Infuse your practice with the spirited frequencies of 528Hz or 639Hz, resonating with the solar plexus and heart chakras

Opening script: "Embrace the energy and spontaneity of your inner teenager. Let each pose and transition be a celebration of your carefree spirit."

Poses to consider:

- Lion's Breath

- Child

- Butterfly

- Twisted Lizard

- Dancer

- Upward Bow

Transitions: Move with spontaneity, allowing each transition to be a celebration of your inner teenager.

Breathwork coaching: Inhale playfulness, exhale inhibition. Let each breath reconnect you with the carefree spirit of your inner teen.

Closing script: "Carry the carefree spirit beyond the mat. Inhale playfulness, exhale inhibition, and let each breath reconnect you with the joyous energy of your inner teen."

Notice Your Thoughts: Developing Mindfulness by Observing and Understanding Your Thoughts

Music: Elevate your awareness with the clarifying frequencies of 852Hz, resonating with the third eye chakra.

Opening script: "As you notice your thoughts, cultivate mindfulness and inner clarity. Let each pose and transition guide you into the clarity of your thoughts."

Poses to consider:

- Half Bow

- Lotus

- Mountain

- Plank

- Chair

- Eagle

Transitions: Move with mindfulness, allowing each transition to be a journey into the clarity of your thoughts.

Breathwork coaching: Inhale clarity, exhale mental chatter. Let each breath guide you into a state of mindful awareness.

Closing script: "As you step away, carry the clarity within. Inhale clarity, exhale mental chatter, and let each breath guide you into a state of mindful awareness."

Now, as we step into the golden landscapes of autumn, we shift our focus to the rhythmic dance between release and renewal. The vibrant leaves gently surrender to the earth, mirroring the beauty of letting go. This chapter promises a journey into the themes that align with the essence of this season.

Chapter 7:

Autumn

Autumn, with its kaleidoscope of earthy hues and the rhythmic dance of falling leaves, invites us to reflect on the impermanence of life. It is a season that beckons us to turn inward, reconnect with our inner selves, and align with the cyclical nature of existence. The 27 themes presented in this chapter are designed to inspire and empower yoga teachers and practitioners alike, fostering a deeper connection with the transformative energies of fall.

Live Your Truth: Embracing Authenticity and Living in Alignment With Your True Self

Music: Introduce a blend of instrumental music with cultural influences to represent diversity. Use 528Hz and 721Hz sounds for the solar plexus and throat chakras

Opening script: "As we step onto the mat, let's embrace the power of self-honesty. Inhale the truth, exhale self-expression. Today, we align with our solar plexus and throat chakras, awakening the courage to live authentically."

Poses to consider:

- Child's Pose

- Mountain Pose

- Camel Pose

- Tree Pose

- Triangle

- Warrior 1

Transition: Flow seamlessly between poses, mirroring the ebb and flow of your authenticity.

Breathwork coaching: Inhale courage, exhale self-doubt. Let your breath reflect your inner truth.

Closing script: "As we conclude, carry your authenticity off the mat. May your truth shine, a beacon guiding you through life's journey."

Find Happiness in the Little Things: Cultivating Joy in Life's Simple Pleasures

Music: 639Hz for the heart. Consider music that brings a sense of joy and celebration.

Opening script: "In the simplicity of autumn, let's discover joy in the little things. Today's practice resonates with the heart, inviting gratitude and happiness into each breath and pose."

Poses to consider:
- Cat-Cow Pose

- Mountain Pose

- Chair Pose

- Tree Pose

- Corpse

- Standing Forward Fold

Transition: Move gracefully, savoring the sweetness of each transition.

Breathwork coaching: Inhale gratitude, exhale joy. Let your breath be a melody of happiness.

Closing script: "As you leave the mat, carry the warmth of gratitude with you. In the little things, may you find boundless joy."

Grow With the Earth: Nurturing Personal Growth in Harmony With the Changing Seasons

Music: 396Hz for the root chakra. Include nature sounds or ambient music to complement the earthy theme.

Opening script: "Rooted in the earth's wisdom, let's ground ourselves in the season of growth. Today, we connect with the root chakra, finding strength in the embrace of the earth beneath us."

Poses to consider:

- Child

- Downward Dog

- Mountain

- Warrior 1

- Warrior 2

- Tree

Transition: Flow seamlessly, embodying the natural cycles of growth.

Breathwork coaching: Inhale stability, exhale growth. Let your breath sync with the earth's heartbeat.

Closing script: "As you stand tall, remember your connection to the earth. May your growth be nurtured by the wisdom beneath you."

Shed the Layers: Letting Go of What no Longer Serves You

Music: 528Hz and 639Hz for the solar plexus and heart. Mix ambient sounds with the suggested frequencies for a calming effect.

Opening script: "In the gentle release of autumn, let's shed the layers that no longer serve us. Today, our practice invites us to make room for new beginnings, resonating with the solar plexus and heart chakras."

Poses to consider:

- Wide-Legged Child

- Pigeon

- Restorative Fish

- Legs Up the Wall

- Fish

- Puppy

Transition: Flow gracefully between poses, shedding the old with each movement.

Breathwork coaching: Inhale release, exhale renewal. Let your breath carry away the old.

Closing script: "As you rise from the mat, feel the lightness of shedding. May you embrace the new with open arms."

Be Curious: Approaching Life With an Open Mind and a Spirit of Exploration

Music: 417Hz for the sacral chakra. Integrate diverse world music or fusion genres.

Opening script: "In the curiosity of autumn's dance, let's explore the depths of our creativity. Today's practice taps into the sacral chakra, awakening the power of curiosity and self-expression."

Poses to consider:

- Krishna

- Eagle

- Pigeon

- Revolved Low Lunge

- Low Lunge

- High Lunge

Transition: Dance between poses, embodying the spirit of curiosity.

Breathwork coaching: Inhale creativity, exhale exploration. Let your breath guide your curiosity.

Closing script: "As you step off the mat, carry the spark of curiosity. May your journey be filled with endless exploration."

Get in Tune With Yourself: Fostering Mind-Body Harmony and Inner Connection

Music: Consider a mix of classical and modern instrumental pieces. Use 417Hz and 639Hz frequencies for the sacral and heart chakras.

Opening script: "As the autumn breeze whispers, let's tune into the symphony of our being. Today's practice harmonizes the sacral and heart chakras, guiding us to know ourselves deeply."

Poses to consider:

- Mountain

- High Lunge

- Cat-Cow

- Camel

- Downward Dog

- Warrior 1

Transition: Move fluidly, becoming one with the music of your existence.

Breathwork coaching: Inhale self-awareness, exhale self-acceptance. Let your breath be the melody of self-discovery.

Closing script: "As you carry the tune within, may your journey be a symphony of self-love and authenticity."

Enjoy the Journey: Embracing the Present Moment and Finding Joy in the Process

Music: Use 639Hz for the heart. Include music that captures the essence of a joyful journey.

Opening script: "In the tapestry of autumn, let's savor the beauty of the journey. Today's practice resonates with the heart, inviting you to love and appreciate every step of the way."

Poses to consider:

- Downward Dog

- Happy Baby

- Sphinx

- Goddess

- Warrior 1

- Warrior 2

Transition: Flow gracefully, enjoying the rhythm of your practice.

Breathwork coaching: Inhale love, exhale gratitude. Let your breath celebrate the journey.

Closing script: "As you step off the mat, cherish each moment. May your journey be filled with love, joy, and gratitude."

Embrace Change: Navigate Life's Transitions With Grace and Resilience

Music: 528Hz for the solar plexus. Incorporate music with dynamic changes to reflect the theme.

Opening script: "As the leaves gracefully fall, let's welcome the winds of change. Today's practice resonates with the solar plexus, inviting us to embrace the transformative power of change."

Poses to consider:

- Dog

- Supported Bridge

- Plank

- Tadpole

- Bow

- Mountain

Transition: Move seamlessly, mirroring the fluidity of change.

Breathwork coaching: Inhale acceptance, exhale transformation. Let your breath be the wind of change.

Closing script: "As you step into the world, may you dance with the winds of change. Embrace the beauty of transformation."

Center Yourself: Grounding and Finding Stability Amidst Life's Flux

Music: 528Hz for the solar plexus. Include calming instrumental pieces.

Opening script: "In the quiet rustle of autumn leaves, let's center ourselves amidst the changing seasons. Today's practice, guided by the sound of 528Hz, invites balance and calmness into our beings."

Poses to consider:

- Easy

- Neck Rolls

- Mountain

- Low Lunge with Eagle Arms

- Seated Circles

- Seated Side Stretch

Transition: Flow gently, embodying the stillness within.

Breathwork coaching: Inhale balance, exhale calm. Let your breath be the anchor in the changing seasons.

Closing script: "As you step off the mat, carry the center within you. May you navigate life's changes with grace and inner calmness."

Connecting to Your Throat Chakra: Expressing Your Authentic Voice

Music: 741Hz for the throat chakra. Integrate vocal-centric music from various cultures, such as African or Asian.

Opening script: "In the crisp clarity of autumn air, let's connect to the essence of our throat chakra. Today's practice invites communication, expression, and the art of speaking our truth."

Poses to consider:

- Fish

- Cobra

- Plow

- Shoulder Stand

- Mountain

- Child

Transition: Flow seamlessly, embodying the fluidity of self-expression.

Breathwork coaching: Inhale clarity, exhale expression. Let your breath be the voice of your truth.

Closing script: "As you carry the resonance of your truth, may your words create ripples of authenticity in the world."

Be Your Own Teacher: Empowering Yourself on Your Yoga Journey

Music: Explore diverse genres that inspire self-trust and empowerment. Use 528Hz for the solar plexus.

Opening script: "As the leaves fall and transform, let us turn inward. In the rhythm of your breath, discover the teacher within. Today, guided by the solar plexus, we embark on a journey of self-trust and empowerment."

Poses to consider:

- Warrior 1

- Warrior 2

- Child

- Cat-Cow

- Mountain

- Tree

Transition: Flow seamlessly, becoming your own guide.

Breathwork coaching: Inhale self-trust, exhale empowerment. Let your breath guide your inner teacher.

Closing script: "As you leave the mat, carry the lessons of self-trust. May you always be your own wise guide on this journey of life."

Focus on the Feeling: Cultivating Awareness of Sensations in Each Pose

Music: Mix genres that evoke a range of emotions. 417Hz and 639Hz for the sacral and heart chakras.

Opening script: "In the dance of sensations, let us turn our attention inward. Today, the sacral and heart chakras guide us to trust the feelings that guide us, honoring the wisdom of our inner compass."

Poses to consider:

- Full Pranam

- Low Lunge

- Lizard

- Twisted Chair

- Humble Warrior

- Pigeon

Transition: Flow gracefully, trusting the ebb and flow of your emotions.

Breathwork coaching: Inhale intuition, exhale surrender. Let your breath be a guide through the realm of feelings.

Closing script: "As you rise from the mat, may you navigate life's journey with the wisdom of your feelings as your guide."

Practice Kindness: Extending Compassion to Yourself and Others

Music: Integrate gentle and compassionate tracks. Use 639Hz for the heart.

Opening script: "In the gentle embrace of autumn, let us cultivate kindness within. Today's practice, guided by the heart, encourages us to lead with love and compassion."

Poses to consider:
- Bridge

- Camel

- Cobra

- Bow

- Sphinx

- Fish

Transition: Flow gracefully, allowing kindness to guide your movements.

Breathwork coaching: Inhale love, exhale kindness. Let your breath be a gentle breeze of compassion.

Closing script: "As you step off the mat, carry the warmth of kindness. May your journey be adorned with acts of love and compassion."

Take Your Time: Moving at Your Own Pace, Honoring the Beauty of Slowness

Music: You can use slow-paced instrumental pieces at 396Hz for the root chakra

Opening script: "In the gentle sway of autumn leaves, let us learn the art of slowing down. Today, guided by the root chakra, we invite you to take your time and savor each moment."

Poses to consider:
- Corpse

- Child

- Cat-Cow

- Downward Dog

- Happy Baby

- Legs Against the Wall

Transition: Move mindfully, embodying the essence of taking your time.

Breathwork coaching: Inhale presence, exhale patience. Let your breath be the guide in the realm of time.

Closing script: "As you step into the world, may you carry the gift of time. May your journey unfold with grace, one mindful step at a time."

Clear the Lens: Gaining Clarity and Perspective on Your Life's Path

Music: 852Hz for the third eye chakra. Incorporate music with clear and precise tones.

Opening script: "In the clarity of autumn's air, let us focus on sharpening our vision. Today's practice, guided by the third eye chakra, encourages us to clear the lens of perception and find clarity within."

Poses to consider:
- Side Stretch

- Head-to-Knee Pose

- Extended Side Angle Pose

- Pigeon Pose

- Easy Pose

- Warrior 2

Transition: Flow seamlessly, embodying the clear path ahead.

Breathwork coaching: Inhale clarity, exhale confusion. Let your breath guide you to a clear state of mind.

Closing script: "As you step into the world, may your vision be sharp and clear. May you see the beauty and truth in every moment."

Sit in Your Silence: Embracing Stillness and Finding Peace in Quiet Moments

Music: You can use calming music, like Asian instrumentals at 396Hz or 852Hz for the root and third eye chakras.

Opening script: "Amidst the rustle of autumn leaves, let us find solace in silence. Today's practice, guided by the root and third eye chakras, invites us to sit in quietude and discover the peace within."

Poses to consider:

- Corpse

- Legs Up the Wall

- Child

- Downward Dog

- Reclining Bound Angle

- Seated Forward Fold

Transition: Move gently, preserving the tranquility within.

Breathwork coaching: Inhale peace, exhale stillness. Let your breath be the whisper of silence.

Closing script: "As you re-enter the world, may the echoes of silence accompany you. May you find peace in every moment, even amidst the noise of life."

Be Open to Opportunity: Welcoming New Possibilities With Openness and Optimism

Music: 417Hz or 639Hz for the heart chakra. Use uplifting and positive music, like Latin instrumentals.

Opening script: "In the ever-changing landscape of autumn, let us open our hearts to new opportunities."

Poses to consider:

- Camel

- Sphinx

- Cobra

- Downward Dog

- Cat-Cow

- Butterfly

Transition: Move gracefully, embodying the openness to new opportunities.

Breathwork coaching: Inhale positivity, exhale resistance. Let your breath guide your openness.

Closing script: "As you step into the world, may you greet each opportunity with a heart wide open. Embrace the positive changes that come your way."

Believe in Your Abilities: Cultivating Confidence in Your Strength and Capabilities

Music: Use empowering tracks with a strong beat at 528Hz for the solar plexus chakra.

Opening script: "In the golden glow of autumn, let us celebrate our strength and abilities. Today's practice, guided by the solar plexus chakra, invites us to believe in ourselves and embrace confidence."

Poses to consider:

- Bow

- Cobra

- Sphinx

- Boat Pose Sail

- Downward Dog

- Camel

Transition: Flow seamlessly, feeling the rhythm of your own abilities.

Breathwork coaching: Inhale confidence, exhale doubt. Let your breath guide your belief in yourself.

Closing script: "As you step off the mat, carry the confidence within you. May you believe in your abilities to navigate the journey ahead."

Choose Self-Love: Nurturing a Positive and Compassionate Relationship With Yourself

Music: Use music that resonates with love and acceptance at 639Hz for the heart.

Opening script: "In the gentle embrace of autumn, let us choose to love ourselves unconditionally. Today's practice, guided by the heart, invites us to celebrate the beauty and love that resides within."

Poses to consider:

- Dancer

- Rabbit

- Bow

- Bridge

- Forearm Stand

- Wild Thing

Transition: Move with love, embodying the essence of self-love.

Breathwork coaching: Inhale self-love, exhale self-acceptance. Let your breath be the melody of unconditional love.

Closing script: "As you leave the mat, carry the warmth of self-love. May you radiate love to yourself and others on this journey of life."

Celebrate the Autumn Equinox: Honoring the Balance of Light and Dark

Music: anything uplifting and calming.

Opening script: "As we stand on the threshold of autumn, let us celebrate the balance of the autumn equinox. Today's practice is a joyful ode to the changing seasons, guided by uplifting and calming melodies."

Poses to consider:

- Sun Salutation

- Downward Dog

- Tree

- Forward Fold

- Chair

- Camel

Transition: Flow gracefully, symbolizing the interconnectedness of all things.

Breathwork coaching: Inhale balance, exhale gratitude. Let your breath harmonize with the essence of the autumn equinox.

Closing script: "As you step off the mat, may the equilibrium of the equinox inspire balance in your life. Celebrate the beauty in the dance of change and the constant ebb and flow of nature."

Find Meaning: Exploring the Depths of Your Yoga Practice and Life's Purpose

Music: 639Hz and 963Hz for the heart and crown chakras. Integrate soulful and introspective tracks.

Opening script: "As the autumn leaves dance, let us explore the profound meaning in our lives. Today's practice, guided by the harmonious tones of 639Hz and 963Hz, invites us to seek purpose and connection in all things."

Poses to consider:

- Mountain

- Tree

- Eagle

- Crane

- Cobra

- Downward Dog

Transition: Flow seamlessly, connecting each pose with purpose.

Breathwork coaching: Inhale purpose, exhale connection. Let your breath guide your journey of finding meaning.

Closing script: "As you step off the mat, may your every step be imbued with meaning and purpose. May your journey be a tapestry of significance."

Untether Yourself: Freeing Your Mind and Spirit From Limiting Attachments

Music: 528Hz for the solar plexus. Include liberating and freeing music.

Opening script: "In the gentle release of autumn, let us untether ourselves from attachments. Today's practice, guided by the resonance of 528Hz, invites us to let go and find freedom in surrender."

Poses to consider:

- Child

- Legs Up the Wall

- Puppy Pose

- Thread the Needle

- Corpse

- Pigeon

Transition: Flow gently, embracing the fluidity of surrender.

Breathwork coaching: Inhale release, exhale freedom. Let your breath guide your journey of untethering.

Closing script: "As you step off the mat, may you carry the lightness of release. May you find freedom in every step, unburdened by unnecessary attachments."

Change With the Leaves: Embracing the Natural Flow of Life's Changes

Music: 396Hz, 417Hz, and 528Hz for the root, solar and sacral chakras. Integrate music with dynamic changes and transformations like Latin beats.

Opening script: "Amidst the rustle of falling leaves, let us open ourselves to change. Today's practice, guided by the melodies of 396Hz, 417Hz, and 528Hz, invites us to let go and welcome in the transformative dance of life."

Poses to consider:

- Dog

- Supported Bridge

- Plank

- Corpse

- Mountain

- Seal

Transition: Flow gracefully, mirroring the fluidity of change.

Breathwork coaching: Inhale acceptance, exhale transformation. Let your breath be the wind of change.

Closing script: "As you step into the world, may you dance with the winds of change. Embrace the beauty of transformation."

Embrace Your Humanity: Accepting and Loving Every Aspect of Your Being

Music: 639Hz for the heart. Include music that reflects human emotions and experiences, like Indian instrumentals.

Opening script: "In the heart of autumn, let us dive into the core of our humanity. Today's practice, guided by the heart, encourages us to feel into what makes us beautifully and authentically human."

Poses to consider:

- Sun Salutations

- Child

- Cobra

- Downward Dog

- Mountain

- Chair

Transition: Flow seamlessly, moving with the rhythm of your own heartbeat.

Breathwork coaching: Inhale authenticity, exhale vulnerability. Let your breath guide your exploration of humanity.

Closing script: "As you step off the mat, may you carry the richness of your humanity. May you embrace the beauty of being authentically and unapologetically human."

Find Peace: Cultivating Inner Calm and Serenity

Music: Integrate calming and serene tracks at 396Hz for the root chakra.

Opening script: "In the tranquility of autumn, let us find serenity within ourselves. Today's practice, guided by the grounding tones of 396Hz, invites us to discover peace amidst the changing seasons."

Poses to consider:

- Easy Pose with Forward Bend

- Standing Forward Bend

- Wide-Legged Standing Forward Bend

- Plow

- Corpse

- Triangle

Transition: Flow gently, embodying the peace that flows within.

Breathwork coaching: Inhale serenity, exhale surrender. Let your breath be the rhythm of peace.

Closing script: "As you step into the world, may the peace within you radiate outwards. May you find tranquility in the midst of life's ever-changing landscape."

Open Yourself to Others: Fostering Connection and Vulnerability

Music: 639Hz for the heart. Explore genres that evoke a sense of unity, for example African beats.

Opening script: "In the embrace of autumn, let us open our hearts to the world. Today's practice, guided by the melodic tones of 639Hz, invites us to give and receive love with an open heart."

Poses to consider:

- Bridge

- Camel

- Cobra

- Bow

- Sphinx

- Fish

Transition: Flow gracefully, allowing the river of love to guide your movements.

Breathwork coaching: Inhale love, exhale compassion. Let your breath be the bridge between hearts.

Closing script: "As you step off the mat, may your heart remain open. May you radiate love, connecting with the hearts of others in the dance of life."

Be Authentic: Living Truthfully and Unapologetically as Your Genuine Self

Music: 396Hz, 417Hz, 528Hz, 639Hz, and 741Hz for the root, sacral, solar plexus, heart, and throat chakras. You can be creative and use diverse tracks from various cultures.

Opening script: "In the symphony of autumn, let us be true to ourselves. Today's practice, guided by the harmonies of 396Hz, 417Hz, 528Hz, 639Hz, and 741Hz, invites us to express our authentic selves with courage and grace."

Poses to consider:

- Chair

- Warrior 1

- Dolphin

- Plank

- Revolved Side Angle

- Side Crow

Transition: Flow with authenticity, moving in harmony with your true self.

Breathwork coaching: Inhale authenticity, exhale courage. Let your breath be the melody of your authentic expression.

Closing script: "As you step into the world, may you wear your authenticity as a crown. May you dance to the rhythm of your own truth, fearlessly and authentically."

As we enjoy the colors of fall and explore themes connected to the season, we're about to move on a meaningful journey. Just as the leaves gracefully release their vibrant hues, inviting us to let go and embrace change, we too stand at the threshold of a transformative practice.

Now, as we turn the page to our final chapter, it's time to step into the realm of endless possibilities. The practice of creating your own theme is an invitation to become the architect of your experience on the mat. Just as the autumn winds carry whispers of change, you have the power to craft a sequence that resonates with your unique essence, personal aspirations, and the needs of those you guide.

Chapter 8:

Create Your Own Theme

This chapter is a beacon for yoga teachers seeking to infuse their classes with personal meaning, elevating the practice for both themselves and their students. This is not merely about selecting random concepts; it's an invitation to discover the power of intention and purpose in every breath, every movement, and every moment shared on the mat.

In the pages ahead, you'll unravel the significance of weaving themes into your classes and learn how to craft sequences that resonate with the core of your being. This isn't just about designing a sequence; it's about curating an experience that lingers in the hearts and minds of those you guide.

Whether you're an instructor looking to breathe new life into your teaching or a budding yogi on the journey to becoming a teacher, this chapter is a compass guiding you to create classes that are not just physical practices but holistic journeys toward well-being.

Are you ready to embark on a path that transcends the ordinary? Let's delve into the art of creating your own theme and uncover the secrets of crafting yoga sequences that are as unique as you are. The mat awaits, and within its sacred space, you have the power to transform lives, starting with your own.

Identifying Your Purpose

As a yoga teacher, the journey begins within. Take the time for introspection, delving into your core values and beliefs. What principles guide your own practice? What philosophies resonate with your spirit? By understanding the essence of your being, you pave the way to craft themes that authentically reflect your inner landscape.

Beyond the personal, consider your role as a guide on the mat. What do you aspire to offer your students? What transformations do you wish to facilitate in their lives? I encourage you to articulate your teaching goals and intentions by selecting themes that align with your mission.

Choosing Themes

Nature serves as a powerful muse for thematic inspiration. Learn to attune yourself to the energies of the seasons—drawing inspiration from the vitality of spring, the warmth of summer, the introspection of fall, and the stillness of winter. Discover how aligning your themes with nature can deepen the resonance of your classes.

Seasons change, and so do the energies within and around us. Explore the art of adapting themes to harmonize with nature. Whether it's the renewal of spring or the reflection of winter, discover how to tailor your themes to resonate with the unique qualities each season brings.

Uncover the alchemy of aligning physical postures with the chosen theme. Learn to sequence poses that embody and express the essence of your theme.

Elevate your teaching by transforming your classes into storytelling experiences. Discover the art of building a narrative through movement, where each pose is a word and each sequence a sentence.

Incorporating Breathwork and Meditation

Breath is the bridge between body and mind. Explore the profound impact of breathwork in amplifying your theme. Learn techniques to synchronize breath with movement, fostering a deeper connection to the chosen concept. Discover how intentional breath can elevate the entire class experience.

Meditation becomes a powerful tool to anchor the theme in the minds of your students. Delve into the art of crafting guided meditations that seamlessly align with and support your chosen concept. Whether it's a journey within or a visualization that complements the theme, meditation becomes the soulful culmination of your class.

Enhancing Verbal Cues

Language is a conduit for energy. Learn the art of selecting words that harmonize with the chosen theme, creating a linguistic landscape that enriches the entire class experience. Discover how to infuse your cues with intention, making every word important to your theme.

Verbal cues are more than instructions; they are threads weaving a narrative throughout the class. Explore the subtleties of creating a storyline with your words. Whether guiding students into a pose or encouraging them through challenges, learn to tell a story that amplifies the essence of your chosen theme.

Personalizing for Your Audience

Every student brings a unique journey to the mat. Explore the art of tailoring your themes to meet the diverse needs of beginners, intermediate, and advanced practitioners. Learn to scaffold your themes, ensuring that each student, regardless of their level, can connect with and benefit from the overarching concept.

Yoga is for everybody and every soul. Discover strategies to ensure inclusivity in your theme selection, fostering a sense of belonging for students of all backgrounds and abilities.

As we stand at the threshold of creating your own theme, imagine the yoga studio as a canvas, and you, the instructor, as the artist ready to paint a masterpiece. This chapter is an odyssey into the realm of intention, purpose, and creative expression—a journey that transcends the boundaries of a standard yoga class.

Just as a painter infuses their art with emotions, and a musician weaves melodies that resonate with the soul, you, as a yoga teacher, have the power to craft classes that linger in the hearts and minds of your students. The mat becomes your canvas, and your words and movements become the brushstrokes that create a unique and transformative experience.

This chapter is an invitation to explore the depths of your own purpose, to align with the forces of nature, and to become a storyteller on the mat. It's an opportunity to elevate your teaching from a series of postures to a symphony of movement, breath, and intention.

So, as you step onto the mat with an open heart and a curious mind, you are about to embark on a transformative odyssey—the journey to becoming an empowered yoga teacher. This voyage commences with a profound exploration and the artful creation of themes that extend beyond the physical postures, resonating not only with your students but also with the very essence of who you are as an individual.

The canvas before you is blank, a metaphorical representation of the vast possibilities that lie within the realm of yoga teaching. It is an open invitation to delve into the depths of self-discovery and creative expression. The first strokes of this artistic endeavor involve the careful selection and crafting of themes that align with your personal values, experiences, and aspirations. This is not just about instructing a series of yoga postures; it is a conscious and intentional effort to infuse your classes with a profound sense of purpose and meaning.

Imagine this process as navigating uncharted waters—an exciting and sometimes challenging expedition into the realms of your own beliefs, passions, and the unique flavor you bring to the practice of yoga. Creating themes gives you the chance to tell the story of your journey, combining elements like mindfulness, self-love, and spiritual exploration into the foundation of your classes.

As you engage in this journey of self-discovery, be prepared to uncover aspects of yourself that may have been dormant or undiscovered. Embrace the opportunity to express your authenticity and individuality, for it is through this process that your teaching becomes a reflection of your own transformative path. Your themes, carefully chosen and passionately delivered, become the vehicle through which you share not just the practice of yoga, but a piece of your own evolving narrative.

May the themes you create resonate not only with the bodies on the mats, but also with the hearts and souls of those who partake in the transformative journey you facilitate.

Class Title:

Duration:

Theme:

Music:

Intention:

1. Opening:

- Grounding/Intention

2. Warm-Up:

- Poses/Movements

3. Peak Sequence:

- Key Poses/Breathwork Integration

4. Cool-Down:

- Relaxing Poses/Breath Awareness

5. Closing:

- Meditation/Savasana/Closing Words

Notes:

Conclusion

This book is more than a guide; it is a manifesto, a declaration of the profound impact a dedicated yoga practice can have on our lives and the lives of those we touch.

As you close the pages of this book, I invite you to take a moment to reflect on your own journey. Consider the path you've traveled, the challenges you've overcome, and the growth you've experienced. The yoga teacher is not born overnight; it is a continuous process of self-discovery, refinement, and resilience.

Our exploration has revealed the complexity of physical, mental, and emotional well-being. You now have the tools to combine the elements of breath, movement, and mindfulness. Your classes go beyond mere sequences of postures; they are experiences that reach the core of holistic well-being.

The 108 preset themes provided in this book serve as the colors in your palette, allowing you to paint a vibrant picture of well-being in your classes and personal practice. Each theme resonates with a different facet of our lives, creating a mosaic that extends far beyond the confines of the yoga mat. You have the power to cultivate mindfulness, foster self-love, and explore spiritual depths through the themes you choose.

In the spirit of empowerment, I urge you to unleash your creativity. The template provided in the last chapter is more than a guide; it is an open invitation to design your own themes, to infuse your classes with the authenticity that is uniquely yours. Your creativity is a force of nature, and when expressed through your teaching, it becomes a catalyst for profound transformation.

As you craft your own themes, remember that there is no right or wrong. This is your journey, and your themes are an expression of your evolving self. Embrace the freedom to experiment, innovate, and evolve. In doing so, you not only enrich your own practice but also offer your students a glimpse into the boundless possibilities of self-discovery.

As we conclude this exploration of empowerment and holistic well-being, I extend my deepest gratitude for joining me on this journey. May the teachings within these pages serve as a guiding light on your path, illuminating the way toward a more empowered, joyful, and transformative existence.

May your practice be a source of joy, strength, and transformation, both on and off the mat. As you continue to evolve as a yoga teacher, remember that your journey is ongoing, and each moment is an opportunity for growth and self-discovery. *Namasté.*

Thank You for Reading!

I hope you enjoyed reading this book and found it valuable and inspiring. Your feedback is incredibly important and helps other readers discover this book.

If you have a moment, please consider leaving a review on Amazon.

Thank you for your support!

References

André, C. (2019, January 15). *Proper Breathing Brings Better Health.* Scientific American. https://www.scientificamerican.com/article/proper-breathing-brings-better-health/

Baptiste, B. (2018, January 24). *Baron Baptiste's Yoga Sequence for Self-Expression.* Yoga Journal. https://www.yogajournal.com/practice/yoga-sequences/baron-baptistes-yoga-sequence-for-self-expression/

Berbari, G. (2018, March 24). *This Yoga Flow Will Help You Let Things Go When Life Gets A Little Too Toxic.* Elite Daily. https://www.elitedaily.com/p/8-yoga-poses-for-release-thatll-help-you-let-things-go-when-theyre-not-serving-you-8579902

Bové, L. (2021, July 27). *How to theme your yoga classes.* Ekhart Yoga. https://www.ekhartyoga.com/articles/practice/how-to-theme-your-yoga-classes

Brower, E. (2016, September 1). *Elena Brower's Yoga Sequence to Create Space + Find Clarity.* Yoga Journal. https://www.yogajournal.com/practice/yoga-sequences/sequence-find-clarity-elena-brower/

Burgin, T. (2023, August 17). *13 Grounding Yoga Poses to Strengthen the Earth Element.* Yoga Basics. https://www.yogabasics.com/connect/yoga-blog/grounding-yoga-poses/

Carroll, M. (2020, December 3). *Yoga Poses to Honor the Winter Solstice: The Dance of Duality.* Theyogawriter. https://www.theyogawriter.com/single-post/2018/12/21/yoga-poses-to-honor-the-winter-solstice-the-dance-of-duality

Chen, C. (2016, May 3). *11 Poses to Ignite Your Second Chakra and Spark Creativity.* Yoga Journal. https://www.yogajournal.com/practice/yoga-poses-ignite-your-second-chakra-to-spark-creativity/

Clark, S. (2018, March 21). *8 Poses to Cultivate Courage and Reduce Self-Conciousness.* Yoga Journal. https://www.yogajournal.com/practice/yoga-sequences/8-poses-to-cultivate-courage-and-reduce-self-conciousness/

Cleveland Clinic. (2019). *Diaphragmatic breathing exercises & techniques.* Cleveland Clinic. https://my.clevelandclinic.org/health/articles/9445-diaphragmatic-breathing

Coco, K. (2018, April 22). *YIN YOGA SEQUENCE TO WELCOME CHANGES IN LIFE.* Swagtail. https://swagtail.com/welcome-life-changes/

Costa, K. (n.d.). *8 Tips for Theming a Yoga Class.* Yogainternational.com. Retrieved February 3, 2024, from https://yogainternational.com/article/view/8-tips-for-theming-a-yoga-class/

Cronkleton, E. (2018, August 15). *How to Breathe and Ways to Breathe Better.* Healthline. https://www.healthline.com/health/how-to-breathe

Cullis, L. (2016, April 7). *Baptiste Yoga: 5 Poses to Access the Power of Imperfection.* Yoga Journal. https://www.yogajournal.com/yoga-101/types-of-yoga/hot-yoga/baptiste-yoga-5-poses-to-access-the-power-of-imperfection/

Fowler, K. (2018, April 18). *16 Poses to Instantly Boost Your Confidence.* Yoga Journal. https://www.yogajournal.com/practice/yoga-sequences-level/beginners-sequences/16-poses-to-instantly-boost-your-confidence/

Freedman, S. (2018, December 13). *This Sequence Will Help You Tap Into the Power of Your Intuition.* Yoga Journal.

https://www.yogajournal.com/practice/yoga-sequences/yoga-for-intuition-poses-to-boost-your-intuitive-powers/

fvckyes. (2022, October 14). *What makes a good yoga teacher?* Reddit. https://www.reddit.com/r/yoga/comments/y3odcq/what_makes_a_good_yoga_teacher/

Giacomini, A. (2018, September 21). *16 Yoga Poses to Spark Inspiration.* Yoga Journal. https://www.yogajournal.com/practice/yoga-sequences/this-months-home-practice-16-poses-to-spark-inspiration/

Goldem, N. (n.d.). *Yoga for All Seasons: Winter.* Gaiam. Retrieved February 3, 2024, from https://www.gaiam.com/blogs/discover/yoga-for-all-seasons-winter

Health Yoga Life. (2021, June 10). *Yoga Poses to Ring in the Summer Solstice.* Health Yoga Life. https://healthyogalife.com/yoga-poses-to-ring-in-the-summer-solstice/

How To Create A Yoga Class Theme (+39 Yoga Themes) – Brett Larkin Yoga. (2020, July 27). Www.brettlarkin.com. https://www.brettlarkin.com/yoga-class-themes/

Indries, M. (2022, March 28). *An Empowering Yoga Practice to Cultivate Your Feminine Energy.* Yoga Journal. https://www.yogajournal.com/practice/yoga-sequences/yoga-practice-feminine-energy/

Lasater, L. (2019, October 14). *Sequence for Silence and Savasana.* Yoga Journal. https://www.yogajournal.com/practice/yoga-sequences/sequence-for-silence-and-savasana/

Lepore, M. (n.d.). *7 Yoga Poses for Better Thinking.* Www.thinkherrmann.com. Retrieved February 3, 2024, from https://www.thinkherrmann.com/whole-brain-thinking-blog/7-yoga-poses-for-better-thinking

Longson, L. (2018, October 30). *Get Grounded: An Autumn Yoga Sequence for Calm and Stability.* Balance Garden.

https://www.balancegarden.co.uk/blog/autumn-yoga-sequence

Maia. (2024, January 15). *Winter-Themed Yoga Poses and Lesson Ideas for Kids*. Kumarah. https://kumarahyoga.com/winter-themed-yoga-poses-and-lesson-ideas-for-kids/

Martell, T. (2022, March 16). *This Yoga Sequence Embodies the Energy of the Spring Equinox*. Yoga Journal. https://www.yogajournal.com/practice/yoga-sequences/yoga-sequence-spring-equinox/

Mitchell, K. (2022). *Yoga Class Themes: Tips, Examples & Implementation | OriGym*. Origympersonaltrainercourses.co.uk. https://origympersonaltrainercourses.co.uk/blog/yoga-class-themes

Pansa, J. (2016, January 27). *A Yoga Sequence to Inspire a New Beginning*. Yoga Journal. https://www.yogajournal.com/practice/yoga-sequences/yoga-sequence-inspire-new-beginning/

Peterson, H. (2021). *Power of the Heart: 10 Heart Opening Postures*. Corepoweryoga.com. https://www.corepoweryoga.com/blog/mindfulness/power-of-the-heart-10-heart-opening-postures

Pizer, A. (2023, July 31). *8 Yoga Poses that Promote Self-Love*. Liforme. https://liforme.com/blogs/blog/yoga-poses-to-promote-self-love

Reid, M. (n.d.). *8 Yoga Poses For Your Crown Chakra*. Www.kelleemaize.com. https://www.kelleemaize.com/post/8-yoga-poses-for-your-crown-chakra

Richards, L. (2020, May 18). *How to breathe properly: Guide and tips*. Www.medicalnewstoday.com. https://www.medicalnewstoday.com/articles/how-to-breathe-properly

Ridout, E. (2021, December 15). *Celebrate the Winter Solstice With This Grounding Yoga Flow*. Yoga Journal.

https://www.yogajournal.com/practice/yoga-sequences/winter-solstice-yoga-flow/

Rodefer, E. (2022, October 30). *What Makes a Good Yoga Teacher? Our List of 11 Top Traits.* Yoga Journal. https://www.yogajournal.com/teach/what-makes-a-good-teacher/

Shain, E. (2019, April 20). *8 Yoga Poses to Celebrate Spring and New Beginnings.* Yoga Journal. https://www.yogajournal.com/practice/yoga-sequences/yoga-sequence-for-spring/

Singh, M. (n.d.). *7 Teaching Tips Every Yoga Teacher Should Know.* Gaiam. https://www.gaiam.com/blogs/discover/7-teaching-tips-every-yoga-teacher-should-know

65 Yoga Themes and Intentions to Transform Your Teaching. (2021, June 3). Yoga Room Hawaii. https://www.yogaroomhawaii.com/blog/65-yoga-themes-to-transform-your-teaching

Smith, D. A. (2021, October 23). *This Gentle Flow Will Help You Make Peace With Stillness.* Yoga Journal. https://www.yogajournal.com/practice/yoga-sequences/make-peace-with-stillness/

Smith, E. (2023, May 14). *Let Love In: 6 Yoga Poses to Open Your Heart.* YogaUOnline. https://yogauonline.com/yoga-practice-teaching-tips/yoga-practice-tips/let-love-in-6-yoga-poses-to-open-your-heart/

Spremberg, D. (2018, February 28). *10 Yin Yoga Poses For Embracing Change.* Dagmar Spremberg. https://dagmarspremberg.com/yin-yoga-embracing-change/

13 Qualities of a Great Yoga Teacher, Plus 5 Tips to Stand Out | ISSA. (2023). Www.issaonline.com. https://www.issaonline.com/blog/post/13-qualities-of-a-great-yoga-teacher-plus-5-tips-to-stand-out

Thompson, E. (2022, September 25). *Recess Break! 10 Yoga Poses Your Inner Child Will Love.* YouAligned™. https://youaligned.com/yoga/inner-child-poses/

Versteeg, S. (2019, April 3). *5 Yoga Poses For Inner Strength.* YogaRenew. https://www.yogarenewteachertraining.com/5-yoga-poses-for-inner-strength/

Ward, L. (2021, December 18). *7 Yoga Poses to Inspire Your Creative Side and Practice Mindful Movement.* YouAligned™. https://youaligned.com/yoga/mindful-movement-yoga-poses/

Will. (2023, March 6). *Yoga Spring Cleaning: The Best Cleansing Yoga for a New You.* MyYogaTeacher. https://myyogateacher.com/articles/yoga-spring-cleaning#

Yoga with Kassandra. (2023, February 17). *7 Yin Yoga Stretches to Help You Slow Down.* Yoga Journal. https://www.yogajournal.com/lifestyle/astrology/yin-yoga-stretches/

Image References

Stock Photo and Image Portfolio by anvinoart | Shutterstock. (n.d.). Shutterstock. https://www.shutterstock.com/g/AnVino

Made in the USA
Middletown, DE
07 October 2024